QUANTUM
SUCCESS

ALSO BY SANDRA ANNE TAYLOR

Secrets of Attraction:
*The Universal Laws of Love, Sex, and Romance**

Guided-Visualization Audiotape and CD Programs

Act to Attract (nine-CD audio seminar and workbook)
Attracting Love
Attracting Success
Cellular Regression: Timeless Healing
Planting Your Destiny Garden
Higher Self, Higher Powers
Relaxation and Memory Release
Successful Weight Loss
Your Sacred Identity

⊕ ⊕ ⊕

*Available from Hay House

Please visit Hay House USA: **www.hayhouse.com**®
Hay House Australia: **www.hayhouse.com.au**
Hay House UK: **www.hayhouse.co.uk**
Hay House South Africa: **orders@psdprom.co.za**
Hay House India: **www.hayhouseindia.co.in**

QUANTUM
SUCCESS

THE ASTOUNDING
SCIENCE OF WEALTH
AND HAPPINESS

SANDRA ANNE TAYLOR

HAY HOUSE, INC.
Carlsbad, California
London • Sydney • Johannesburg
Vancouver • Hong Kong • New Delhi

Published and distributed in the United States by: Hay House, Inc.: www.hayhouse. com • **Published and distributed in Australia by:** Hay House Australia Pty. Ltd.: www.hayhouse.com.au • **Published and distributed in the United Kingdom by:** Hay House UK, Ltd.: www.hayhouse.co.uk • **Published and distributed in the Republic of South Africa by:** Hay House SA (Pty), Ltd.: orders@psdprom.co.za • **Distributed in Canada by:** Raincoast: www.raincoast.com • **Published in India by:** Hay House Publishers India: www.hayhouseindia.co.in

Editorial supervision: Jill Kramer • *Design:* Tricia Breidenthal

Library of Congress Cataloging-in-Publication Data

Taylor, Sandra Anne.
  Quantum success : the astounding science of wealth and happiness / Sandra Anne Taylor.
     p. cm.
  ISBN-13: 978-1-4019-0732-7 (tradepaper)
  ISBN-10: 1-4019-0732-6 (tradepaper)
  1. Success. I. Title.
  BF637.S8T284 2006
  158--dc22

                            2005036680

                 ISBN 13: 978-1-4019-0732-7
                 ISBN 10: 1-4019-0732-6

                 10 09 08 07   6 5 4 3
                 1st edition, May 2006
                 3rd edition, February 2007

                 Printed in Canada

FOR MY WONDERFUL CHILDREN,
VICA AND JENYAA TAYLOR.
YOUR LAUGHTER IS THE
MUSIC OF SUCCESS TO ME.

CONTENTS

INTRODUCTION

Countdown to Success

Everything changed for me when I was introduced to quantum physics nearly 20 years ago. The principles of energy and consciousness opened my eyes to a world of possibilities that I'd never been aware of before. Since that moment, I've been sharing these ideas with people from all over the world and all walks of life. They've found, as I have, that the patterns of the natural world can be applied to any situation to bring about amazing results.

This science is liberating because it gives *you* control over your future. It's empowering because it allows you to determine the direction of your destiny. No matter what you may have experienced in the past, when you learn how to tap in to these amazing Universal forces, you'll arrive at the real source of success.

Sci-finance

Most people believe that the circumstances of their lives are based on random and uncontrollable occurrences, such as their status or family income. But this idea misrepresents reality and disempowers us completely. The truth is, we direct our life experiences through our interaction with the laws that govern nature.

There are several energetic patterns in the physical world that have powerful applications to humankind. In fact, the science of personal energy and the mechanics of consciousness are the two most important natural factors affecting the outcomes of your goals. Once you actively employ these elements within your life, you'll see profound changes taking shape.

You may have heard it said that "you achieve what you believe" and "that which you focus on expands." While these statements ring true, they're often relegated to the category of idealistic and somewhat impractical philosophy. But in reality, significant natural principles lie behind these concepts, compelling us to look more closely at the science behind them.

Researchers of quantum physics have discovered that everything is made up of vibrating strings of energy. What was once considered to be solid matter is really composed of pulsating, energetic vibrations, which human will and consciousness have influence over. They shape the destiny of each individual, as well as the entire species. In fact, your future is taking shape right now!

It's what you *do* with your consciousness and energy that determines all the outcomes that you experience. This truth is so empowering that its realization will change your life. Even if you've never been aware of it before, the Universal Laws of Attraction impose their influence in every aspect of your existence, including your career, finances, and relationships.

In quantum physics, the uncertainty theory reveals that you live in a state of unending possibilities that are of your own making. The world exists in a constant state of flux where even a small shift in energy can create an immediate and far-reaching change in reality. Although most of the power in the Universe isn't visible, it can still be used to great affect. You may not be able to see an atom, but you can certainly witness the effects of an atom bomb—and your personal unseen vibrations have very dramatic effects, also. But to take control of the power there, you must be willing to explore a new frontier and take a journey through inner space.

Leaving the Future Behind

Many people feel as if they're on a treadmill: constantly on the move but going nowhere. They're tired of running from work to home, from meetings to appointments, with all their time spent on unending tasks and unfulfilling engagements. They consistently turn from one relationship to another and one project to the next, always hoping that the new gambit will bring what they're looking for. They feel empty and stuck, and they long to be free. They're desperate for change, but they just don't know how to make that happen, so they keep repeating the same old patterns over and over again.

If this sounds familiar, and each new disappointment seems like just another trip down memory lane, take heart. You *do* have the power to create a different life. In fact, quantum physics reveals that you're at the very center of a world of unlimited power and potential. You don't have to go through your days just getting by and feeling dissatisfied any longer. The Universal Laws can completely turn things around.

I've used these principles in every aspect of my own life. They've helped me go from being a high-school teacher to a counselor to an international speaker and author. After two failed marriages, I'd pretty much given up on love, but I decided to apply the Universal Laws to that pursuit also. Within a year, I met my current husband, a truly supportive, loving, wise, and humorous man who has enhanced my life beyond words.

But perhaps my most amazing experience in terms of these astounding precepts has been the story of my two wonderful children. People called my husband and me crazy for wanting to adopt two unrelated preteens from a Russian orphanage. But I knew that the laws of energy and consciousness were absolute, and if I took the right steps in employing their powers, we'd attract the very best kids—and we did!

It was a long and involved process, an extraordinary story that's so remarkable in the occurrence of "magical" events that it would take another book to tell about it. But everything turned out great, and it changed all of our lives in immeasurably happy ways.

I've also taught these principles for nearly 20 years to individual clients and in seminars all over the world. Since the beginning, I've heard countless success stories from people who've applied the techniques to both their private and professional lives. One man who started a software business in his garage was offered nearly $7 million for his company. Another fought depression and anxiety to get out of a low-level food-service position and open his own restaurant and catering business. He's become so successful that he's been asked to create a national franchise.

In Australia, where I speak every year or two, I was approached by a woman pushing a stroller. She told me that a couple of years previously she'd taken my seminar on how to attract love. At that time she was alone, but she very much wanted a family. After learning about the laws and then implementing the techniques, she met the love of her life. She'd come back to thank me and to introduce me to her beautiful new baby.

I receive e-mails and letters from all over the world with similar tales. It's so gratifying to hear the success stories of so many individuals achieving what they desire: getting promotions or new jobs, finding love, or starting a business or a family. Some have even reported losing weight and looking younger!

Whatever these people were working on, they were all empowered by their understanding of the science of success. They saw within their own lives that a shift in energy and consciousness could make anything happen. While some of the particular techniques discussed here may sound familiar, it's the Universal power and energy available all the time that's the source of our solutions. And you, too, can tap in to it and make your dreams come true.

The previous patterns of your life may have left you unhappy, and you may be gazing into the future without much hope, but you can leave that gloomy outlook behind. Your journey to a new, happy future can begin right now!

Journey to Success

An important part of your self-exploration is keeping a Success Journal. The word *journal* originally meant a written record of the experiences on a journey. Your pursuit of success is a voyage in itself, and your written record will help you get from here to your ultimate destination. Your process will take you through many stops along the way, and your entries can act as a personal road map, keeping you on track and redirecting you toward your goals.

As you go through the chapters, there will be several suggestions about what to record in your Success Journal, but the first entry you need to make is actually about where you want to end up. So take some time now to draw up your wish list, writing down everything that you desire. Whether it's a million dollars, a new home, a blissful romance, a raise, or an entirely new career, take note of every single thing that your heart dreams of. Continue to add to this list whenever you think of something else you long for.

INTENTIONS

When you've completed this initial catalog, turn every item on it into a specific intention. For example, if a million dollars is on your wish list, you'll write: "I intend to be a millionaire." If you're looking for a new romance, write: "I intend to attract a wonderful, caring partner. I'm drawing real, long-lasting love to me right now." As you'll see, an important part of your journey will be to consistently turn your desires into intentions and your beliefs into affirmations.

This focus is also a very important part of your connection with the Universal laws. It combines with your consciousness and your vibration to create the greatest influences over your personal destiny. It's so significant, in fact, that you should investigate it often. Whenever I start a new project or engage in a new activity, I try to consider what my intention is at that time. This creates a focus for the pursuit I'm engaged in, and it fine-tunes the energy around it. Even if it's just starting a new day, a clear purpose goes a long way toward keeping you on track.

AFFIRMATIONS

Affirmations are easily dismissed by some people, yet they can be a very dynamic part of energy production. If you're not consciously occupied with such positive thoughts, it's likely that you're unconsciously engaged in negative ones.

At the end of each chapter, you'll find a few pertinent affirmations. Pick the ones that resonate with what you need most, read them often, and make sure that you include some basic statements of self-acknowledgment no matter what you're working on. Repeat the sentences as you look in the mirror, and try rephrasing them using the second and third person (*you* and *he* or *she*). When you say them right out loud, your acoustic energy amplifies your electromagnetic vibrations and doubles their power.

Change your affirmations as you begin to work on new issues, adding any that will help you focus on your positive intentions concerning yourself, your goals, or your world. Affirm yourself and your life every day, and the Universe will bless you in countless positive ways.

Quick Change

Quantum physics demonstrates that great shifts of energy can occur in a single moment. This is true for your life, too—at every second, you're participating in the creation of your destiny. The energetic realm is always waiting to respond to your vibrations, so get ready to step into the future with new tools and more power than you ever thought you had. This is one science experiment you don't want to miss!

I've called this book *Quantum Success* not only because of the scientific principles involved, but also because of what the quantum world represents. This reality happens on a cellular level, yet the effects are nonlocal, impacting things in far-distant space and often having no regard for linear time. When you've achieved *quantum success,* you'll find that you feel happiness down to your very cells, and you'll experience joyous achievement in every moment.

This book is divided into seven parts, each section having one less chapter than the part before. This is a countdown of sorts, moving through the seven most important influences on the experience of personal success. From the Seven Laws to the Six Powers, all the way down to the One Path to Success, your application of these techniques will bring increasing momentum to the pursuit of your dreams.

So start your countdown now: Make these principles an active part of your daily life, and your success will take off like a rocket! You'll soon find that your lifestyle, career, personal relationships, and virtually everything else will begin to change. You'll see that nothing's impossible when you employ this amazing science. Your soul is connected to the powerhouse that charges all of creation, and it's time to open yourself to that Universal current—that pulsating energy that directs your destiny. When you do, you'll find, as I have, that your life has been blessed beyond your expectations.

✦ ✦ ✦

PART I

THE SEVEN UNIVERSAL LAWS OF SUCCESS

You live in a miraculous world. Truly wonderful things are happening all around you, and you can bring that enchantment to all that you do and all that you'd like to achieve! If you feel that your desires have been elusive up till now, you need to know that a world of power and energy is waiting to help make your dreams a reality.

What seems like sorcery is actually the workings of the energetic world; what appears to be mystery is really the result of scientific patterns. Consciousness and energy are in perpetual motion, vibrating within and around you in an endless celebration of cause and effect—and this "magic" part of the process isn't even visible to the human eye. The *unseen* power of the Universe is no longer a mystical reference; it's a scientific truth.

Such is the nature of the quantum world, pulsating with power and endless possibilities! You're a vibrating force in the workings of this world, a creative consciousness that directs both your own destiny and that of all humankind. You are—at this moment—engaged in an exquisite act of personal and global creation. When you take control of the cosmic energy within, you align yourself with the Universal Laws, a source that will allow you to create a wellspring of happiness, success, and value beyond belief!

⬥　⬥　⬥

Chapter 1

THE LAW OF MANIFESTATION

The First Universal Law of Success

---

*". . . the primal cause is mind. Everything must start with an idea.
Every event, every condition, every thing is first an idea in the mind . . ."*
— Robert Collier

The mechanics of your mind reveal fascinating possibilities—not merely in the capacity to work out complex problems and learn new information, but an ability that transcends logic and actually moves into the realm of physical creation. This is the power of your consciousness, and it's the source of your destiny creation.

⚖ The first Law of Success, the **Law of Manifestation,** demonstrates how things come into being. In quantum physics, consciousness creates reality—and this applies to your personal world as well.

Modern science explores many theories of consciousness-created reality. One is cosmological, explaining how the Universe came into being. It says that our world is far too complex to have reached this stage of development merely through a random series of coincidental events, so it must be the result of conscious intention. Another theory has to do with how physical reality is constructed out of the raw material of the Universe, and yet another explores how our individual consciousness chooses one of the infinite possibilities that are available to us at each moment of time. Even the theory of observer-created reality, which has to do with how particles and waves are measured, indicates that intention and consciousness are very real forces.

The science behind these quantum-physical theories is intriguing, but it's your *personal* reality that we'll examine here. The individual application of observer creation reveals that what you notice about yourself becomes present. Think about this for a moment: What do you tend to note about yourself? Are those self-observations negative or positive? What kind of reality do you think that you'll come up with based on them?

These are significant questions, and it would be helpful to answer each one in your journal. But this is only the beginning where your destiny manifestation is concerned, since *your consciousness creates your reality.* To understand how, it's important to find out what your "consciousness" is and how it acts as a creative force in your life.

If you want to see this power, all you have to do is take a look around you. Setting aside the discussion of Higher Consciousness–created reality and what you see in the natural world, it's easy to see the power and the presence of personal consciousness in your daily life. As I pause right now, I witness it everywhere: The spirit of a street artist from St. Petersburg, Russia, reveals itself to me in a painting that hangs on my wall; the consciousness of Mozart plays to me from my CD player; the energy of Charles Dickens speaks to me as I read myself to sleep at night; and the inspiration of a stained-glass artist and dear friend shines for me as sunlight streams through one of her creations. The consciousness of a furniture builder supports me, and a home builder protects me. In these and a million more ways each day I'm influenced by the creative force of others, and I am a witness to what humans can create.

When we add the natural world into the mix and open ourselves to the real fullness of consciousness-created reality in every sense of its meaning, we can see its beauty and force everywhere. From the smallest pebble on a dirt road to the expanse of the midnight sky, from a child's paper airplane to a nationally computerized power grid, it all began in the power of the mind. This is the fundamental reality of all manifestation: Everything exists in consciousness first. And while not all of it produces beneficial results, every bit of it produces something. Consciousness created the World Trade Center and also destroyed it.

✵ In terms of your personal life, your success—or lack of it—manifests in your consciousness first. If you can look around you and see failure and difficulty, that's a product of your mind. If you see abundance and achievement, that's a force of your own, too. Everything that you'll ever manifest is in the boiling pot of your conscious energy, creating the concoction that you'll later call your life. The Law of Manifestation is clear: If your consciousness creates your reality, you simply can't manifest anything that doesn't exist fully formed inside you first. You can't experience success without an unconflicted knowledge of what that looks and feels like first.

What's Your Consciousness Creating Now?

The phrase "Your consciousness creates your destiny" by no means translates to mean "You consciously create your destiny." The fact is that most of us are completely unaware of how we script the circumstances we find ourselves in. In truth, most people don't even know *that* they create their situations. They perceive life as a series of random events that, for the most part, aren't of their own making. Very rarely does it occur to them that what they experience is something they've unknowingly set up.

For this reason, one of the first requirements of the Law of Manifestation is to investigate exactly what it is you're focusing on. The following questions are designed to help you get in touch with this important aspect of your destiny creation. While you'll be exploring the many layers of manifestation in the next chapter, this exercise will help you start to become more aware of your consciousness direction.

JOURNAL FOR SUCCESS

Answer these questions in your success journal. Review them often to investigate your consciousness creativity on a regular basis.

- Generally speaking, what are the things you're most conscious of—that is, what do you tend to think about the most? Are you more conscious of what you have or what you lack?

- What's your most important career goal? How much time do you spend each day consciously focusing on its *success?*

- What's the most prevalent habit, pattern, or even addiction in your life? How much time do you spend each day engaging in this habit? How conscious of it are you when you're not doing it?

- Do you tend to focus more on the positives of your day or the problems that come up? Does your thought process tend to be more negative or positive?

The answers to these questions are important indicators of your consciousness direction. You have within you the power to design your destiny the way you want it; you're at work on it right now. But just as an architect can't design a masterful building with his eyes closed, you can't become the architect of your dreams until you open your eyes to your choices.

Becoming Conscious

Do you ever stop to notice what you're thinking about? How often do you really consider the consequences of your choices *before* you make them? There are many people who are clueless about why they do what they do—or even what it means. They move through whole decades at a time, reacting out of some unconscious and largely unconsidered approach to life. These are what I call the "consciousness zombies," trudging through life day after day in an unaware state. They follow their habits and react out of emotion, doing what's required and not much more. But if this sounds like your own approach in the past, don't worry. You do have the power to awaken from the ranks of the undead. You can choose a different, higher, and brighter consciousness and move on to a better life than you've ever experienced—perhaps even better than you've ever dreamed of.

> ✳ Consciousness is always a choice. It's the choice to bring your awareness to the present moment, the decision to see and prioritize that which is truly important, that which is genuinely honoring and value enhancing in your life. Your constant question must be: "What am I focusing my consciousness on now?" And the question that follows is: "What might this consciousness be creating for me?"

I have a client who readily admitted that she spent most of her day thinking about food. Surprisingly, she was only a few pounds overweight, but she was very honest about her obsession with wondering what, when, and how much she was going to eat each day. Because she struggled to control this, she exercised regularly, and had never been really obese. She lost or gained a little, but it didn't change the fact that she was always unhappy with her weight.

She had similarly bad feelings about her career, where she made just enough money to get by in tedious jobs that were always just okay, while doing a little freelance writing on the side. She hadn't realized that neither her weight issues nor her job problems were ever going to change until she began to consciously focus more on her career than she did on food.

We worked on letting go of her obsession and creating a sane approach to eating. She began to affirm self-acceptance at any weight, and she also raised her consciousness about her career priorities. I told her that every time she thought about food, she had to engage in some sort of positive thought or specific action concerning her career. This shifted both her focus and her motivation, and it was just what she needed to get results. In time, she not only lost weight, but her freelance-writing career became so successful that she was able to quit her job and make twice as much money doing something she loved.

You, too, can take control of your own destiny manifestation. To shift your consciousness creation, you need to be much more aware of the positive than the negative—and of your value and priorities. Choose to focus your thoughts on the good things that you already have, as well as those that you're going to attract. Always take deliberate action in the direction of your goals instead of engaging in unconscious reactions and distractions.

In the next chapter, we'll discuss specific techniques that will enable you to make a total consciousness shift, but you can start awakening to your options right now. Remember, if you don't like what you're creating, you must change what you're conscious of. When you catch yourself focused on the negative, you need to know that your mind is creating negative results. Shift that focus no matter what it takes, and you'll soon see the powerful and positive outcome that a truly optimistic consciousness can create!

AFFIRMATIONS TO ENHANCE MANIFESTATION

- *Every day I am becoming more aware of what I prioritize and what I tend to focus on. I prioritize my goals. I focus on all that I have to value.*

- *I am choosing to be more and more conscious of what I have to appreciate in my life.*

- *I am conscious of my resourcefulness, my creativity, and my power to create a great destiny.*

- *I know that my consciousness creates my reality. I always choose an optimistic mind-set.*

- *I consciously choose hope, joy, and peace in my daily life.*

◈ ◈ ◈

Chapter 2

THE LAW OF MAGNETISM

The Second Universal Law of Success

---

*"Every person is surrounded by a thought atmosphere. . . .
Through this power we are either attracting or repelling.
Like attracts like and . . . we attract just what we are in mind."*

— Ernest Holmes

While the first Law of Success concerns what you *create,* the second one, the Law of Magnetism, concerns what you *attract.* These two forces together have the greatest impact on your destiny: The first has to do with the power of your consciousness; the second has to do with the power of your energy.

There are many patterns of energy at work in the world today. Amazingly powerful yet unseen forces have very real and predictable outcomes. For instance, if you key in the numbers of a very specific signal to your cell phone and then press the "talk" button, that sequence will be directed by a satellite thousands of miles away to the appropriate recipient. Another phone will ring, and the energy of your voice will be bounced back and forth, allowing you to have a clear conversation even if you're a great distance away from the other person. If you push a button on a remote control, a signal will be sent to a box in the corner of the room and a television picture will form—complete with sound—again transmitted from a far-distant source. Modern CAT scans and MRIs use energy to create images of the body. Microwaves cook food, sensors ensure security, and lasers remove tumors.

The list of ways in which modern humans have harnessed, directed, and utilized energy is almost endless. All of the above phenomena—and countless more—have very significant physical results, but the influences aren't limited to medicine, communications, and technical gadgetry. The energetic workings of the Universe impact each and every one of us in ways that most people are never aware of—even to the point of individual experiences of happiness and success.

⚖️ The **Law of Magnetism** says that we can only attract the same kind of energy that we put out about ourselves. It's based on the quantum-physical principle that everything—including every person—projects this power. In fact, the Universe is filled with vibrations that scientists call "strings" of energy. It moves within us, from us, and all around us literally all the time. Whether we're aware of it or not, each of us is a part of a vast exchange and expansion of this force that takes place in the Universe every moment of every day.

Our personal energy moves outward from us and connects with others of like resonance, determining both whom and what we'll attract in life. Each of us is like a little radio station, constantly broadcasting signals about our self and our life. The people and situations that match those signals are the ones that will tune in to us and be drawn into our life experience. In truth, what we call *chemistry*—whether it's romantic or professional—is actually more of a resonance, a matching of signals and personal vibrations. So if success is what you're after, it will be very important to understand how your energy is created—and what it may be broadcasting about you even now.

Your Energetic Calling Card

In the Victorian era, calling cards were used to announce the arrival of a visitor or friend, and letters of introduction were sent ahead to pave the way and help someone new connect with others of like society. It was a formal process, but one which let the recipient know that the bearer was well connected and highly regarded.

Your personal resonance does much the same thing. Long before you arrive at an experience in life, your energy has sent messages about you to the people you'll be interacting with. It announces you to every-one, revealing that part of you that others relate to on an unconscious but very compelling level: your energetic nature. So if you don't like the society or circumstances you've attracted so far, or if you've had difficulty finding the success you desire, you'll need to change what you put into your energetic calling card.

Luckily, since this frequency is something that you produce your-self, it's also something that you can change. Once you figure out what makes up your vibrational resonance, you can take active steps to improve your magnetic frequency and change all that you attract.

There are three major ways that your personal resonance is created:

1. Through your emotional energy, or the vibrations of your feelings

2. Through your cognitive energy, or the vibrations of your thoughts

3. Through your physical energy, or the vibrations of your body

Let's take a closer look at the first two methods on this list.

THE EMOTIONAL BROADCAST

Your emotional resonance is by far the most powerful expression of yourself. Your daily feelings broadcast loud and clear signals about who you are and what you expect from the world. If you're chronically fearful, for example, you project that and will only attract more and more situations that will cause you to be afraid. If anger is predominant, you're sending out signals that you expect hostility—and that's exactly what you'll get.

But if you choose a lighter, happier attitude, you broadcast the message that you expect the world to be a joyous place, and both your energy and your expectation will bring more of that to you. If you have confident and peaceful feelings about yourself, they'll send out a very magnetic vibration, attracting people and experiences that bring an even deeper sense of serenity to your life. This is your resonant reality; what you send out will most certainly come back to you.

Your predominant feelings energize your destiny creation by virtue of their powerful presence in your heart and mind. The more emotionally charged an experience or issue is, the more power it generates. For this reason, a shift to more positive sentiments is a basic requirement of the Law of Magnetism. It's an energetic truth that the quality of your emotional life will determine the caliber of your life in general. In this the law is strict: The Universe will return your own joy, love, and happiness to you; and it will return your fear, anger, and unhappiness as well.

But where do emotions come from? What's the source of this powerful energy that you engage in all the time? Underneath every single emotional experience is a stimulating source. Whether the feeling is anger or love, misery or joy, depression or excitement, boredom or bliss, every blossom or thorn of sentiment has one originating seed—and that seed is thought.

THE THOUGHT'S THE THING

The second way that you project your energy out into the world is through your cognitive power. Your thoughts rarely stop, so they're continually churning out vibrational messages in your energetic field. And since they're also the source of your emotional energy, they're doubly important in your pursuit of success.

Thoughts of confidence bring feelings of hope, while those of inadequacy bring feelings of despair. Which is more likely to attract wonderful outcomes to you? The positive results you're looking for can only come from peaceful emotions and positive thoughts.

If you're like most people, the process of thinking may seem rather random and spontaneous, something that you just experience rather than decide on. Maybe you've never been taught to think positively, or maybe the direction your mind takes depends on the situation you're in or the people you're with. One thing's for sure: If you look around you and find your life wanting, the Universe is telling you to take control of your thoughts!

Most negative thinking is based in one of three fears:

1. Fear of the future
2. Fear of rejection
3. Fear of failure

Fear of the future can range from fleeting worries that something may go wrong to wild anticipation of personal catastrophe, including thoughts such as *What if the meeting doesn't go well? What if I lose this account? What if I get sick or die?*

Fear of rejection runs the gamut from nagging concerns about being judged to utter panic about being abandoned. People who have these kind of thoughts are often self-critical or even self-loathing. Thoughts such as *I'm not good enough, I'm not capable,* and *I'm not worthy* invariably lead to fears such as *What if my spouse leaves me?* or *What if I get fired?*

All fear is toxic to the energy of achievement, so it's inevitable that fear of failure creates the energy of a self-fulfilling prophecy; those who see themselves as unsuccessful can only draw defeat. These negative thoughts are your greatest obstacles to genuine happiness. They destroy optimism and increase worry and frustration, two miserable vibrations that attract miserable results. It's often said that your life moves in the direction of your dominant thought, and your energy is the reason why.

⊕

My client David lived his life with a pervading sense of fear. He was constantly worried about what other people thought, judging himself and assuming that others would do the same. Although he could function well enough to keep his job, his fears always prevented him from moving forward. He was smart and creative, and he often had good ideas but never had the confidence to present them. After 20 years at the same job, he found that he could make enough money to get by—but unless he made some changes, he'd never earn any more.

David knew that he had to do something. Fear was his predominant emotion, and worries of judgment and rejection were his primary thoughts. His emotional/cognitive energy was constantly churning out signals of gloom and doom, causing him to attract more of the same. But although he'd been living like this for quite some time, he was determined not to stay stuck in this pattern.

He made a list of all the things he worried about and a corresponding list of positive options that would change his emotions, as well as his energy. He persistently worked on letting go of the old worries, and he consciously chose to replace them with peaceful, trusting, and confident conclusions instead.

Bit by bit, David became less fearful and much more relaxed. He began to feel positive emotions he hadn't felt in years, emotions such as peace, hope, and even happiness. The process of shifting his thoughts in order to calm his feelings took some time, but eventually he could actually sense his personal energy changing, too. He became confident, more productive, and willing to take greater risks—and his employer began to take notice.

Within 18 months of learning about the dynamics of energy creation, David got the first of several promotions. A few years later, I received some pictures and a note from him. His company letterhead indicated that he was now a vice president, and the pictures that he sent were of his newly acquired vacation home on Hilton Head Island, South Carolina.

In less than four years, he'd totally reversed decades of energy stagnation. And because of the work he was willing to do to shift the resonance of his own thoughts and emotions, he was finally able to achieve the lifestyle that he'd deeply desired for so long.

TEE for You

Whatever your situation in life, you don't have to stay stuck in the old patterns any longer. It's time to understand your own Thought/Emotion/Energy connection. This is what I call your TEE Equation. The TEE Equation represents how the first level of your energy is created, and this is the formula:

$$Thoughts + Emotions = Energy$$

The power of your most dominant thoughts plus the force of your most frequent and intense emotions equals the resonance of your personal energy field. This is the pulsating vibration that broadcasts your individual signal and determines everything you attract to your life. If you're dissatisfied with what you've drawn in—either personally or professionally—you must work on changing your energy. And as even basic math students know, you can't change the second half of an equation without also changing the first half. Just as you can't add two plus two and get anything but four, you simply can't add negative thoughts to negative emotions and get anything but negative energy—and eventually negative results.

JOURNAL FOR SUCCESS

In order to get a handle on this aspect of your destiny creation, keep a record of your thought patterns in your journal. (If your journal is too big to carry all the time, just keep a little notebook with you.) As you jot down your most commonly experienced ideas, you'll find that you tend to think about the same issues over and over, repeating the same old conclusions about them.

After you've written down what's occupying your mind, describe the emotions being created. If you find that negativity is the predominant energy of your thoughts and feelings, then create the intention to at least let them go. When you catch yourself thinking something negative, just affirm: *I can let this go. I do not have to think this way any longer. I choose to release worry and judgment, and I choose to engage in trust instead.*

When you feel an unpleasant emotion taking over, stop for a moment to investigate what you were thinking about just before having that feeling. Then go to the source of the problem again by releasing the thoughts. You can also reduce the power of the feeling by physically moving, doing some deep breathing, shaking out your muscles, and just affirming: *Release. Release. Release.* If you can, try to replace those negative thoughts with more optimistic conclusions, but at the very least choose to let them go.

⊕

It's extremely important to become aware of the energetic frequencies that you send out each day. Instead of responding unconsciously, broadcasting cognitive and emotional energy that you really don't want to represent you in the energetic realm, you must become very aware of your options in thoughts and feelings. It may seem difficult at first, but it's crucial in projecting the energy of success. It's very empowering to know that you yourself are sending out the waves of information that define you to the world—and that determine what you get back from it. These energetic vibrations are within your power to alter in any given moment. By transforming just one predominant negative thought, you'll make a major shift in your energy. And as you continue to make these shifts within, everything around you will begin to change, including the outcomes of your desires.

⊕

AFFIRMATIONS FOR DYNAMIC MAGNETISM

- *I energize my life with positive thoughts and peaceful emotions at every opportunity. It is my choice.*

- *I am now choosing a new optimistic attitude about myself, my life, and my future.*

- *I am becoming more and more conscious of the kind of energy that I create each day. I choose positive energy in all that I think and do.*

- *Through my own energy, I have the power to make my life better in every way. I know that as I choose to create healthier, happier thoughts and emotions, I will attract even more joyful results.*

- *I know that I have all of the talent and resources I need to magnetize all that I desire.*

⊕ ⊕ ⊕

Chapter 3

THE LAW OF PURE DESIRE

The Third Universal Law

"Desire is possibility seeking expression."

— Ralph Waldo Emerson

The next two laws are driven by your intentions or motivations. Underneath every drive and every desire is the real reason for your pursuit. Although you may not even be aware of what it is, this will either accelerate or block your desired outcome by virtue of its energetic nature.

In order for you to align yourself with the powerful forces of the third Universal Law, your intention must be pure—not manipulative, fear based, or desperate. In other words, your motivations must be genuine, healthy, and honoring to yourself and others. This law and the next one are all about *why* you're going after your goals in life. So if you've never thought about it before, now is the time to consider why you do the things you do.

⚖️ The **Law of Pure Desire** says that when you're driven by a pure intention—one that's free of fear, doubt, and desperation—you can be certain of a beneficial outcome. Freedom from fear shifts the energy of your motivation from negative, resistant vibrations to positive, receptive ones. You'll go from energies of longing and desperation to those of hope and expectation, two vital components of this law.

Motivations that are founded in fear or filled with doubt can only create a dark energy around your desire. Such emotions originate in neediness, sending out waves of repulsive energy. Fear's negative signal is clear, and the message is: *I'm incapable. I'm undeserving. I'm lost.* With this kind of resonance, the only things you can attract are situations and people that bring painful evidence that your negative conclusions are true.

The emotions of fear and doubt eclipse all of the positive-energy boosters that you could project, and sabotage the important components required by the third Universal Law. The engine of pure desire is ignited by an honest and honoring intention, but it's fueled by the positive energies of hope, excitement, enthusiasm, and belief. Your longing must be surrounded by these feelings if it's going to move freely forward in the Universe.

Hope empowers you. It lifts the soul and opens the heart, and it's the source of your enthusiasm and excitement. Without hope you can't get excited about your desire—or keep your passion high enough to keep going when faced with obstacles.

Excitement and enthusiasm are like amplifiers on a stereo system, energizing the process of your desire. But you won't maintain these powerful emotions if you don't have genuine hope and the true belief that your dream can and should become a reality for you. In addition, the loss of hope can be one of the biggest causes of depression and despair, two dark energies that nothing bright or beautiful can get through.

That's what happened to my client Francine. She was employed in a large flower shop that had been owned by the same family for three generations. Working alongside the grandchildren of the two brothers who'd opened the shop several decades before, Francine knew everything that there was to know about flowers. She was the establishment's premier arranger and decorator, and she was in charge of many important accounts, including those of movie stars and politicians. She was a great "people" person and had long lists of clients who requested her by name.

When she first came on board with the second generation of owners, she'd hoped that her excellence in sales and presentation would cause her to move ahead in the company. But when the third generation came to work in the family business, it became painfully clear that she was in a dead-end job. In spite of their lack of skill and experience, the founders' grandchildren soon started receiving the raises and promotions that Francine had been looking forward to.

Although this should have come as no surprise, she felt deeply hurt and soon became hopeless about ever getting ahead. She lost all enthusiasm for her job, and her performance and productivity started to suffer. Before too long, she was warned that her work would have to get back up to par or she'd be let go.

Francine was in the depths of depression when she came to see me. I soon found out that when her original hope for advancement was lost, she constructed the belief that she'd never get ahead. We immediately started working on changing her negative energy, and I also explained how she'd trapped herself in a web of conflicting intentions.

Calming Conflicting Intentions

It's not uncommon for people to have two very different feelings about their desires. On the one hand, you may tell yourself that you want to be successful—that's the first driving intention. On the other hand, a defeating experience or a limiting belief may lead you to believe that it isn't possible—and that also becomes an energetic intention.

In this case, your desires are both desperate and *dis*parate (or opposite), and these intentions fight each other in the energetic realm. Intellectually, you're expressing: *I want; I desire.* Yet your emotional energy is screaming out: *It's hopeless! It can't happen!* Which beliefs will the Universe serve?

Energetically, your negative emotions tend to be more highly charged, and therefore, they're much more compelling in the process of attraction. The more despondent and desperate you become, the more the Universe will have to honor your intention to keep those difficult energies in your life.

This is precisely what happened to Francine. When she started at the flower shop, she believed in herself and had hope about the future. But over time, factors completely beyond her control caused those feelings to change. She had a sense of being defeated that was so negatively emotionally charged, it actually became her new intention.

But Francine was far from beaten. It took some work, but we were able to uncover her original belief in herself—and in her abilities. We also created new hope in the form of a new goal: She devised a plan to open her own flower shop. Setting aside a little money from every paycheck, she also pursued getting investments from some of her clients. Although this seemed very difficult at first, Francine was able to muster up the courage that she needed by keeping her eye on the prize.

With determination and perseverance, she was able to win. She now owns three shops, and her long list of prestigious clients is longer than ever before.

If you find yourself feeling defeated, you must rekindle your hope and redefine your beliefs. Without positive expectations and confidence in your success, you, too, will be caught in the web of conflicting intentions, trapped in an inertia of energy and activity that can only lead to empty results. It's not just a cliché, it's an energetic truth: No matter what your desired intention may be, if you allow yourself to feel defeated, you will be.

From Desiring to Deserving

It's not enough to desire something; it's also necessary to know that you deserve it. This is the next important component of the Law of Pure Desire. For your wishes to be pure, you must genuinely believe that you're worthy of what you want.

Your sense of deserving is usually something that you're taught when you're very young. It's given to you in how you're treated (or mistreated), in judgment or in praise. It's fundamentally tied to the amount of approval and affection that you received when you learned who you are. Even now, you're holding on to the conclusions that you made long ago about what you should get and why, and those beliefs are an influential part of your present process of attraction.

JOURNAL FOR SUCCESS

To better understand the real source of your feelings of worthiness and deserving, answer the following questions in your journal:

- In what ways have you been told—by your parents or others—that you don't deserve?

- Do you believe that you don't measure up in some way, that there's something in you that's lacking? If so, what is it?

- Do you feel that you have to *do* something, *prove* some-thing, or in some way *be* something different in order to be worthy? If so, what?

What do your answers reveal about you? If they say that you're undeserving, you need to know that they aren't demonstrating your truth. In fact, your sense of unworthiness comes from someone else's reality, fear, or need for power. And whether that "someone else" was a parent, teacher, social influence, or anybody else, you don't have to embrace their version of the truth any longer. Your real deserving isn't based on what you've been told by your parents or anyone else. Your worthiness isn't determined by how much money you make, your college degree, how old you are, or what you weigh. Instead, it originates in your Divine legacy.

✳   Always affirm that you deserve the best. Your value and worthiness are gifts from your original source. They come from your Divine heritage, the unconditionally loving energy of your eternal parent. With this as your source, your merit never varies and never falters; there's no condition to fulfill, nothing you have to do. As a child of God, you've always been—and always will be—truly deserving of all the wonderful things that the abundant Universe has to offer.

I recently counseled a client who was having some trouble at work. She was overloaded with responsibilities and didn't get the acknowledgment or the remuneration that she felt she deserved. I suggested that she begin to saturate herself with just a few affirmations repeated many times each day, including: *I deserve respect; I deserve to be happy; I deserve to be treated well.*

She called me a few weeks later, elated about how much better she felt. In addition, she'd gotten a good evaluation at work, a letter of commendation, and a nice raise!

It's now time to redefine yourself—and your worthiness—according to the fundamental truth of who you really are: an eternally loved child of God. Write some releasing statements in your journal to counter the toxic assumptions you uncovered by answering the earlier questions, and add some affirmations about deserving unconditionally. Let go of any of old conditions or distortions that don't support this new understanding, because these limitations are the prison that restrict your accomplishments. When you free yourself from that prison, you'll be free to let go of even more—and able to receive all that you desire.

When You Want It, Let It Go

It may sound like a cliché, but no amount of need or desperation will help you hold on to anything. It only creates severe energy limitations that you'll have to break free of eventually. Ridding yourself of such needy beliefs and conditional worthiness are the rudimentary steps in achieving the greatest liberation of all: freedom from attachment, the final component of the Law of Pure Desire, which is accomplished through the act of surrendering.

By doing so, you're giving up neither the goal nor the desire. Instead, you're surrendering your attachment—your desperate need to make it happen. It's impossible to have a pure desire when you're feeling desperate, because you're motivated out of fear rather than trust. But loosening your grip is the ultimate engagement in trust, both in the future and in yourself. It acknowledges your ability to create happiness for yourself no matter what happens. The real necessity of this faith-filled attitude becomes alarmingly clear when you investigate the next law, which shows that desperation and urgency will only sabotage your intention to achieve.

AFFIRMATIONS FOR PURE DESIRE

- *I am a worthy and valuable person, deserving of wealth, abundance, and real happiness.*

- *I pursue my goals to enhance a wonderful life, one that I make more and more happy every day.*

- *I know what I want. I know that it is available, and I am excited about the bright future that I'm creating for myself even now.*

- *I know that I deserve good things and great experiences.*

- *Every time I look in the mirror, I affirm and acknowledge my value and my deserving.*

⟡ ⟡ ⟡

Chapter 4

THE LAW OF PARADOXICAL INTENT

The Fourth Universal Law of Success

"The quantum field is just another label for the field of pure consciousness or pure potentiality. And this quantum field is influenced by intention and desire."

— Deepak Chopra

While surrendering is just one of the components of the Law of Pure Desire, it's the energetic axis around which the fourth Universal Law revolves. This principle reveals exactly what happens when we allow urgency and need to become our major motivations. The desire for success is a natural and healthy endeavor, but it's our emotions around *why* we want it that determine its energetic nature.

Trust is an easy, fluid vibration that brings results; desperation is a broken, agitated vibration that stops them cold. When it comes to our pursuit of success, where does our fear come from? It originates in our dissatisfaction with what we have and who we are. We've become a "must-have" society: We see something advertised and we've got to get it. We notice our friends with a new item, and we have to possess it ourselves. We become absolutely driven by dissatisfaction when we don't have what we want, and we're willing to go into debt, lose time with our families, and work unending hours just to have more and more.

But what happens while we're desperately waiting to get what we want? We're projecting a terribly unattractive energy, because not only do we feel dissatisfied, but we also feel deprived. We're constantly obsessed with what we lack—so much so that we become envious when we see others who have the "more" that we long for. Someone who owns a $100,000 home might drive by a $300,000 property and feel poor, but the person who owns the more expensive place could easily see a $600,000 home and also feel bad.

The process goes on and on up the "must-have" ladder—and think of the energy such negative emotions create! Your personal energy field often vibrates with palpable agitation, longing, and despair. You may be sending out such an unsettled and unattractive broadcast that the Universe can't possibly respond with anything positive in return. This is the unyielding truth of the fourth Universal Law: *You're bound to push away the very thing that you're desperate to have!*

⚖ The **Law of Paradoxical Intent** reflects the Law of Magnetism in warning that you'll only get a return of your own negative energy. If you're desperate to make something happen, that repulsive vibration will push it away, turning away the very people and situations that might bring your desired outcome. Your desperation, therefore, creates the paradox—or the opposite—of your original intention, leading you to failure instead of success.

The Universe wants you to achieve all that you desire, and when you align yourself with the Laws of Success, it will do everything in its power to help you on your way—but desperation and urgency are deal breakers. This isn't because the Universe wants to prolong your yearning. In fact, just the opposite is true: It wants you to enjoy your life and engage in a different, higher vibration *now*—and stop waiting for some vague happiness to come in the distant future. The best energy happens when you let go of urgency and engage in trust, when you rid yourself of despair and choose peace in the present instead.

You simply can't be happy when you're living in dissatisfaction. When you're obsessed with what you don't have, you draw even more lack; you forego present contentment by setting up a list of goals that you have to have in order to be happy in the future.

In fact, until you have those things, you feel a nagging sense of *un*happiness. You feel as though something's missing, and you can't relax until you fill that void. Instead of enjoying your life and valuing what you have, you spend your time longing for more and constantly striving to get it.

This is a very serious mistake where the laws of energy and consciousness are concerned. *When you give away today's happiness to embrace misery about tomorrow's uncertainty, you shut down your willingness to receive. You shift from a mentality of appreciation to a consciousness of lack and need—and when you make that choice, you lose your power to succeed.*

This is no light matter. What happens when you filter everything you have through wanting something else? You set yourself up for failure by projecting a very unattractive energy of misery. Your need for something else to make you happy will always cause you to perceive your present situation as just not good enough.

Think about the feelings that come from obsessing about what's wrong with your life. Despair, grief, and longing are highly charged emotions, and they attract very difficult results. This abrasive energy is what sabotages your success. It's an irresistible force, and there's no way to get around the power of this law. If you pump out a broadcast of despair, your efforts will only draw back desperate situations and deeper feelings of hopelessness.

The inescapable truth is that *all* of your feelings are charged with positive or negative vibrations. The uplifting ones create flow and wonderful results, while unhappiness creates blockage and problematic results. But you can change your emotions (and your resonance) by switching what you think and what you focus on. You must let go of urgency and engage in thoughts of trust in order to open the doors of magnetic attraction. Shift your concentration from what you lack to all that you have to appreciate in order to create a consciousness of success.

Obsessing about what's missing in your life actually causes you to channel your energy into missing more! And if you're always complaining about what you don't have, it will only create more to whine about.

You need to put your passion into experiencing how you *want* to feel *right now* so that you can magnetize more of that sensation in the future. This is called vibrational entrainment, and it's a must for being in harmony with this law. Think about the appreciation that you'll have at the fruition of your goals, and choose to feel that gratitude for what you have in your life right now.

Getting Past the Paradox

Many people find letting go of urgency to be very difficult because they've attached so many emotional experiences to the hoped-for outcomes of their desires. They worry about whether they can handle it if their dreams don't ever come true; they fear that their desires are out of reach, and they'll never be able to accept that. But when you're engaging in these energies of Paradoxical Intent, the underlying predominant thought about your goal is: *I can't be happy without this.* And with that as your central belief, the inability to be happy actually becomes your reality.

This is what happened to me when I was looking for a publisher for my first book, *Secrets of Attraction*. I had been teaching the principles of quantum physics and romantic attraction to clients seeking relationships for many years with amazing results. Eventually, I started teaching the ideas in seminars, and everywhere I went people asked me where they could get a book on the subject. I didn't know of anything out there that applied the natural laws to romantic relationships, so I decided to write one myself.

I put together a small self-published book that I gave to my clients and sold at my seminars, but people started buying copies for their friends and asking if they were available anywhere else in the country. When the demand kept increasing, I decided to look into getting it published.

That decision spawned a great deal of emotion within me, rekindling a long-held desire. The truth is that I'd wanted to write since I was about 12 years old. At that time, I'd read a book about a teenager living in East Berlin after the Second World War. It was full of pathos, yet touched with humor; it made me laugh and cry, and the printed word had never before reached me in that way. I made the decision then that I wanted to write something that would touch people's lives.

For this reason, I became very excited about getting my book published, but that wasn't the only emotion that came over me. I was also filled with anxiety and urgency about making it happen. I rewrote and edited the small volume that I'd self-published and added an outline for several more chapters to be put in the proposal. I actually had no trouble getting agents—but they certainly had trouble finding publishers.

My first agent was very enthusiastic, certain that she'd get a sale right away. She sent it to the "big" publishers in New York City, and they all had pretty much the same reaction. It was dismissed as just another book about love, rejected because "there are already too many relationship books out there."

This was depressing because I knew that in spite of the great number of books on love, not one of them had addressed the quantum physics of attraction! Almost every week I got a new rejection, and I found myself going deeper and deeper into despair. After being turned down about a dozen times, my first agent said that she had nowhere else to go, so I got another one, who tried another half-dozen publishers—with exactly the same results. In time, she gave up, too.

At first, this sent me into a spiraling depression. My childhood dream of being published seemed to be on the skids. I wallowed in self-pity for a while, but I finally realized that I was engaging in the energies of Paradoxical Intent. In spite of my hope, I'd unknowingly embraced the belief that I couldn't be happy if I didn't make this happen. I was in the middle of conflicting intentions, so the book was going nowhere, and I was getting more and more miserable each day. I knew I had to do something about this!

Every day, I meditated on releasing my paradoxical intentions. I had to let go of the desperate need, but every time I affirmed that it would be okay if I didn't get published, I started to cry. I realized that I was grieving for the potential loss of my dream, but I absolutely had to get back to being happy in the present, so I just allowed myself to go where this process led me. I meditated each day for several weeks, allowing myself to mourn, continuing to release the need.

In time, I was able to genuinely surrender. I came to the conclusion that I'd continue to submit my book to publishers myself, but if in the end I was meant only to self-publish and sell at my seminars, then I'd do so joyfully and see the value in that experience alone. I'd pursue my dream but live with gladness! I shed no more tears, because I had truly let go.

The interesting thing about the Law of Paradoxical Intent is that truly and finally letting go of the desperation is what brings the results—and my case was no exception. Within a few months of really surrendering, I met someone who suggested that I send my book to Hay House. At first I dismissed this possibility, mainly because I thought that it had already been submitted there; in the stream of disappointing rejections, I'd lost track. But upon finding out that that wasn't the case, I realized that the idea truly appealed to me, because Louise Hay had been such a dynamic influence on my life. Her books got me through some very difficult times, and her songs of affirmation were a lifesaver after my father died, so I decided to give it a try.

The process took several months, but since I'd really let go of the urgency, I didn't have the same anxiety as before. In fact, I was so relaxed that I even forgot I'd sent it in. A few months later, though, I learned that my book had been accepted—and I was ecstatic!

The dream of being published had come true, but that was only the beginning. I now realize that Hay House was the company I was meant to be with, the one I resonated with the most. As depressed as I was over those rejections, I understand that I was being protected by the Universe. In the past few years, I've met several people who were published by those other companies, and none of them has gotten the personal care or genuine support I've found at Hay House. I'm working with the most wonderful people in the business: genuinely loving and intent on bringing messages of hope, purpose, and peace to the world. I feel as if I have a personal relationship with everyone there.

In addition, Hay House publishes my books all over the world. I've received countless letters and e-mails from throughout the U.S., Australia, England, Ireland, Singapore, Germany, India, and even Russia and Albania—all from people who wanted to tell me how these principles changed their lives. Those messages mean more to me than I could ever say; they're the manifestation of a desire I've had since I was 12 years old. But I'm convinced that none of these wonderful things would have happened if I hadn't been rejected by those other publishers first!

That process of submissions and rejections took nearly two years, and I was miserable until I finally let go; but now I know what a blessing that really was. Sometimes the Universe doesn't give us exactly what we want when we want it, because there's actually something better down the road. It may be just a happier outcome, or it may be more helpful for our personal growth or for our process in learning how to trust and let go.

In my case, all of these reasons were true. I'm now certain that *not* being chosen in that first year led to a far better professional outcome for me, but even more important, it gave me the opportunity to deal with my own issues of urgency and control. I had to face my own paradoxical intent head-on, and I had to learn to live in trust and *self-established* happiness. It was consistently choosing a present joy that brought the results I wanted—not the other way around!

> ⚖ The **Law of Paradoxical Intent** points out the under-lying paradox of personal achievement: You can get what you want by knowing that you don't need it to be happy! It forces you to shift your focus from a desperate intention to a peaceful pursuit. Never send out the energy that you're willing to wait to be happy—just that you're willing to wait for the goal. Needing a particular achievement before you can live with peace and joy creates a desperate energy that's absolute poison to the resonance of success, so be clear about your intentions and fearless in your motivations. Pursue your goals because you want them to enhance an already happy life, not because you'll be miserable without them.

When it came to getting my book published, I'd built an entire network of desperate needs without even knowing it. I'd invested my value and even my identity in making it happen, constructing a set of catastrophic outcomes if it didn't. I saw it as an end to my childhood dream—and even as a potential death to my professional happiness. I felt that I'd never again be able to define myself as a writer. But none of this was true, because I was already a writer, already engaged in my childhood dream, and I could choose to be happy while working on my goal. My value was secure, and I was in charge of my own self-definition.

I had to remind myself that *success doesn't depend on any one event.* I had to get back to my pure intention: wanting to write in order to share information that I hoped would help people's lives. None of the other things that had seemed so important really mattered, and yet they were all taken care of as soon as I let them go!

JOURNAL FOR SUCCESS

Use your journal to investigate your list of desires. Answer the following questions to find out what your intentions really are:

- What are the underlying *needs* that may be poisoning your process? If you obsess about your need for your goal, you're focusing both your energy and your consciousness on what's missing in your life.

- What are you making your goal really mean? Never let your goal be about defining or saving yourself or making you happy. Pursue it for its own sake. Make the choice to define and save yourself—and make yourself happy—all at the present time.

Be patient, and trust in the Divine timeline. You live in a Universal tapestry where the picture of your destiny comes together according to the threads of your energy, consciousness, and intention. Let yourself weave your future with positive energy; creative consciousness; and pure, unconflicted intention about all things. Never obsess about only one option or solution, and let the desperation go. When your major goal is to live with optimism and trust, your other desires will be met.

AFFIRMATIONS TO RELEASE PARADOXICAL INTENT

- *I know that the Universe is abundant; all that I desire is available to me.*

- *I release desperation. I relax and live with patience, persistence, and peace of mind.*

- *I am letting go of lack and choosing to see only the value and blessings in my life from now on.*

- *I release urgency and live with trust. I know that as I let go of need, I attract my desires to me.*

- *I am practicing the art of surrender. I trust and truly let go.*

⊕ ⊕ ⊕

Chapter 5

THE LAW OF HARMONY

The Fifth Universal Law of Success

"Keep your thoughts and feelings in harmony with your actions. The surest way to realize your purpose is to eliminate any conflict or dissonance that exists between what you're thinking and feeling and how you're living your days."

— Dr. Wayne W. Dyer

In quantum physics, Bell's theorem of nonlocality demonstrates how the action of one particle here can affect the action of another particle separated by a great distance. This is no less true on a personal level, because we live in a Universe where all things are connected. Nonstop energy vibrates within and around us all of the time, connecting us with each other and with the constant flow of Universal energy and events. When we're in harmony, we move into an unending stream of blessings and abundance that is active everywhere in the world. But when we're *out* of harmony, we take ourselves out of this bountiful current and stagnate on the riverbed, watching the blessings go by.

In this way, our harmonizing energy is the key to the magical phenomenon of synchronicity, which is that place where energies are so perfectly aligned that a world of fantastic possibilities opens up. It provides that blend of surprising coincidences that sparks real results. When this happens, we find just what we need in the right place at the perfect time: People show up who can help us along, information is given to us just when we need it, and inspiration seems to come out of the blue. Harmony is the confluence of currents where intention meets outcome in almost mystical ways. But it isn't magic, and it's not random. Harmony is all about alignment—aligning energies, consciousness, and even intentions.

⚖ The **Law of Harmony** says that when you consciously choose to create balance and align yourself with the Universe, your intention and energy open the floodgates of Universal abundance, allowing you access to all the insight, power, and blessings that the world has to offer. In order to achieve this sublime state, your energies must be in tune with all the vibrational sources within and around you. Align your energy with yourself, others, and the Universal flow.

Self-Harmony

All laws—and all solutions—start with the self. The key to harmonizing with yourself is establishing balance in your thoughts, emotions, and activities, which is achieved through your daily choices. The way you live your life—from your seemingly inconsequential thoughts to your most momentous decisions—will determine the amount of harmony in your personal energy.

Balanced thoughts aren't scattered or worried; they're calm, centered, and focused on the task at hand. This mental state starts with self-acceptance and moves on to equanimity with the vagaries of life. It may sound strange, but the kind of equilibrium that creates harmony comes from staying centered in two seemingly opposite intentions: taking complete responsibility and letting go of control.

Real self-responsibility means that you're 100 percent accountable for the quality of your life. You're in charge of your thoughts and emotions and the outcomes that you create. This may seem like a difficult task, so it's important that you see it more as a process. We're always in the midst of living, creating, and attracting. When we make more honoring choices in our thoughts and activities, then our frequency rises and our consciousness shifts. As time goes on, our higher choices become more spontaneous and encourage even greater harmony.

One of the best ways to jump-start this harmonic process is to intervene in your self-criticism. Balanced thoughts vibrate with love—even if the subject of those thoughts is yourself. Self-acceptance is the key to a higher consciousness and more attractive energy. *Don't be hesitant to stop the self-criticism; you can't be both in harmony and in hatred with yourself.*

You can't be in the Divine flow if you hate His creation, and you can't be in harmony with others as long as your thoughts are telling you to fear or control them. This is absolutely crucial to both your consciousness and your energy changes. To live in balance with the world and tap in to that magical river of abundance, you must be in harmony with yourself first.

PEACEFUL PRIORITIES

Begin by seeking a peaceful mind and heart, because all blessings flow from them. This isn't just some simplistic "positive-thinking" theory; it's absolute energetic truth. The more conflict that you experience in your thoughts and feelings, the more discord you'll attract in the outside world.

The most harmonic—and most successful—emotions are love, peace, acceptance, and an enthusiasm for your own life. If you can't learn to bring these core emotions into a prominent place in your daily existence, then you'll continually be striving, with very little to show for it. To avoid this, you need to get back in balance. Your cognitive center *must* be self-acceptance, and your emotional center *must* be self-love.

This kind of peaceful foundation makes it much easier to balance your personal activities, both in time and priorities. Although life often requires your attention in many areas, such as career and family, you may tend to put most of your energies into one concern and sometimes let the others go.

No matter how natural this seems, there's an inherent energetic problem in unbalanced priorities, because you're sending out signals that say you're willing to give up something important to you. These are clear vibrational messages that can only attract people and situations that will require you to give up even more. And if you consistently put *yourself* last, you'll only find yourself coming in last again where the fulfillment of your desires is concerned. There's no getting around it, *the Universe always returns your self-priority to you.*

Harmony in action displays a healthy respect for yourself, your loved ones, your career, and your own personal goals. It's a balancing act, to be sure, but it's well worth the effort. To create the highest harmonic resonance, you need to become truly conscious of how you spend your physical and emotional energy.

If your life is overburdened with endless tasks and you're running around from appointment to appointment, your vibration will be agitated, and you'll attract difficulty and turmoil from others. If your days are spent in the constant distraction of indulgent or addictive activities, this state of being can shatter your harmonic resonance, interrupting what could be fluid movement toward your dream. When you're out of balance, you're out of harmony, and your vibrations are out of tune with the Universal flow.

The harmonic choice is one of tranquility—that is, peace over conflict, trust over fear, and value over judgment—and you can make this decision at every opportunity. Release the tumult in your mind and let go of the fear in your heart. Allow yourself to choose peace, trust, and value instead. Close your eyes, let go, and breathe deeply . . . and feel the shift in consciousness that this creates.

JOURNAL FOR SUCCESS

Use your journal to release your negative thoughts. If you're feeling depressed, write down what you're thinking, and then write a more positive assumption. If you're fearful, affirm that you're switching to trust; if you're angry, use your journal to write about it. This will help you consciously create a greater peace in your emotions. Ventilate your raw energy, and then release the situation to the Universe. Bless it and *truly* let it go.

Harmony with Others

Harmonic resonance begins with the self, then vibrates outward to connect with every other living being. A beautiful vibrational symphony occurs when people are in harmony with each other. You're at the center of that music, and through it you can create beautiful music in every part of your life. But in order to be a part of the glorious sound—and not just sitting in the audience—you must harmonically align your own energies with those of others.

To achieve real harmony, you must arrive at a place of equal acceptance for yourself and others, neither seeking their approval nor denying them yours. This is absolutely essential if you want to remove yourself from the destructive energies of conflict. You can't enlist help from the Universe if you're working against it, so your intention must be to seek unity instead of separation and to acknowledge similarities instead of differences. This isn't just an idealistic worldview; it's a fundamental necessity if you truly want to create the energy to succeed.

Your view of others can't be extricated from how you see yourself. This is a primary part of your personal reality and consciousness. You can't consider the world to be an arena of constant competition without developing a fear-based approach to the pursuit of your goals. As long as you see others as a potential threat to your happiness, you're destined to live in dread and act out of desperation and urgency.

But when you know that *you* are the source of all your solutions, no one can be a threat to you. Living in the higher energies of love and acceptance attracts people who support rather than threaten you. The fact is that in your refusal to accept others, you actually give your power to them. Your energy says, "You have the ability to make me angry or afraid; you have power over me."

But when you make the choice to accept others, you regain your strength. You take control of your emotions and your energies, creating a higher, more peaceful consciousness, one that aligns with the flow of Universal intention. Your choice to accept others demonstrates that you're willing to work together to bring harmony to yourself, each other, and the world—so the more acceptance you have, the more influence you have in the energetic realm. Refusing to accept others not only reduces your power, it actually invites people and situations that will challenge you even more.

Hatred sends out hostile jabs of jagged energy, a resonance that may succeed in hurting others but doesn't stop there. Those barbs of negative vibration snatch up even more negativity from the Universe, gathering momentum and returning far greater hostility back to you. Even if you do so only for your own sake, you must let go of judgment and move past the fear, choosing love and acceptance instead.

Real harmony is achieved when you perceive others with compassion—in other words, when you take yourself out of your experience and imagine yourself in theirs. As more and more people choose to see their shared humanity and connected consciousness, their empathy widens the harmonic flow. This creates a profound and joyous energetic unification, a harmony of understanding that raises your own vibration—and that of everyone involved.

Harmony with the Universe

There's no limitation as to when or where your energies vibrate; there's no time or space within this Universe where your influence isn't felt. All that you do, say, and think moves outward from you in a frequency that has your name on it. In time, it will blend with other similar wavelengths, and those accumulated vibrations will then come back. Whether you draw good or bad toward you will depend on the kind of energies you match.

Harmony with the Universe begins when you connect with the source of the Universe itself—that great Consciousness that created all reality. If you truly want to harmonize your energy with every positive vibration in the world, this is all you have to do: *Connect with Divine Consciousness.* It's present all the time and closer than you think.

It's interesting how people want to dismiss or even resist this powerful force when it comes to applying it to their personal pursuits. Perhaps Divine presence is a foreign concept, evokes fearful memories, or is too abstract—or dogmatic. Whatever the reason, many individuals have a real resistance to calling upon this power, and as a result, they cut themselves off from the major source of their solutions. Whether you want to call this grand creative Consciousness God, Loving Source, Creative Force, or just Universe, it's up to you. All that matters is your undeniable connection to it.

✴ You're a sacred soul and heart, existing as a manifestation of Divine Intention. The Higher Intelligence of all creation vibrates within and around you at all times. The more you align your own energies with this all-powerful heartbeat, the more you move yourself into the flow of Universal blessings. The more you genuinely acknowledge this part of your identity—on both a conscious and energetic level—the more clarity you'll bring to all that you do. When you live in harmony with the loving intention of the Universe, you see clearly, intend purely, and act creatively.

Start to acknowledge this power within by affirming: *I am one with the Loving Source. I connect with the Divine Presence in all things; I acknowledge the Divine in myself and all people. I attract endless blessings from this all-powerful, all-loving Source, and I am grateful.*

MEDITATION: YOUR SACRED CONNECTION

This process will help you harmonize your energies with the Universe. Do this as you go to sleep, or take a few minutes out of your day to just relax and remind yourself of this most loving Force within your life. If it's easier, you can read the script onto a tape and then play the recording as you're falling asleep. Just let yourself focus on the words, and if your mind wanders, gently bring it back to your intention to feel the Divine connection deep in your heart.

Gently visualize the sun's light and warmth flowing through you, making you feel relaxed and tranquil. Deep within, you begin to notice a very powerful presence that has a brilliant source of light all its own. This is the beacon of Divine love bringing you a sense of calm security and filling your heart center with sublime peace. This place is the still point inside, the connection where the all-loving spirit of the Divine embraces and enfolds you in unconditional, perfectly loving light.

Feel this light; breathe in this light; be this light. Allow yourself to experience the energy of Divine love filling you up. Like an eternal well, an unending fountain of illumination fills you with wisdom and joy. Every drop brings clarity and calm, and every vibration brings encouragement and love.

This is the blessed realization of Divine presence, an ever-present gift from the perfect, eternal Source. There's never a time when this perfect light can't be felt or when God's power and presence cannot be invoked. Allow yourself to match the radiant energy vibrating in your own sacred heart—your heart with the Divine heart, your love with Divine love, your intention with Divine intention. This is your sacred connection . . . willing, waiting, and available to you at all times, in all places, for all things. Open yourself to its wonderful energy; know that this loving Presence is with you every day.

Your choice to harmonize with yourself, others, and the loving energy of the Divine casts a magical spell on all the areas of your life. It's the center of synchronicity, the source of miraculous energy that turns conflict into peace and hardship into happiness. Return to this tranquility whenever you get the chance.

AFFIRMATIONS FOR LIVING IN HARMONY

- *I always take responsibility for my thoughts, my emotions, and the quality of my life.*

- *I lead a balanced and happy life. I choose harmony now.*

- *I accept myself; I accept others. I acknowledge the Divine light within us all.*

- *Abundant wealth and happiness flow freely through the Universe, and I deserve to receive all that I desire.*

- *I am one with the Universe. I open myself to the flow of love and blessings all around me.*

◈　◈　◈

Chapter 6

THE LAW OF RIGHT ACTION

The Sixth Universal Law of Success

"We must be the change we wish to see in the world."

— Mohandas K. Gandhi

The Law of Right Action and the Law of Magnetism are closely connected. They both work on the exchange of energy, but there are some subtle differences. The latter deals mostly with how you treat yourself, while the principle you'll explore in this chapter not only includes that idea, but also extends to the treatment of others. This can be an interesting dilemma, because many people mistakenly believe that they can't prioritize both concerns effectively. They think that in order to treat yourself well, you have to be selfish—or to treat others well, you have to sacrifice yourself. But the Law of Right Action indicates that this doesn't have to be the case.

Your energetic output accrues, and all of it—whether it's directed toward yourself or others—creates a kind of destiny bank account. Every thought or action you engage in, every interaction with another— whether it's good or bad—becomes a part of your investment. If you only buy in to negativity, then that's what will pay out. This is true for every action you take, whether it relates to yourself or others.

45

⚖️ The **Law of Right Action** says that your energy is self-perpetuating in the world. Value, honor, and dignity will increase in your life to the same degree that you promote them in the environment around you. On the other hand, if your own actions work to tear down the value, honor, or dignity of others, then in time that destruction will return to you. According to this principle, there's one core question that you must ask yourself about every choice: "Is this honoring to myself and others?"

This is the pivotal point of all of your energetic options. Throughout your life, you're always making choices that will either enhance your sense of honor or deplete it. This is true in your daily decisions, chronic self-talk, and interactions with others. Your days are filled with unending options, and the choices that you make will be energetically responsible for directing your destiny either toward happiness or disappointment.

The energy of honoring is one of the most magnetic and attractive frequencies that you can broadcast. When you choose it, you can feel it in your gut and emotions; but when you make a dishonoring choice, you can sense that something's wrong. Even if things temporarily turn out well, it just doesn't ring true. Although there are no hard and fast rules defining the difference, you'll know it in your heart. Every time you think a thought, make a decision, speak a word, or take a course of action, you'll know inside whether or not you're projecting the kind of honoring energy that will bring value back to your life.

I once had a client named Casey who worked in middle management for a large computer-programming company. She had seven people who reported to her on a daily basis. She relayed her team's results to her supervisor, who then went on to report to the big boss. Casey worked very hard as a team leader, but her goal was to move up the chain of command.

Not long after she assumed her position, she found that her supervisor had been changing some of the data on the reports before they were sent to the boss. At first it seemed to be insignificant, but it still made Casey uncomfortable, although she was hesitant to say anything.

She didn't like confrontation, and her supervisor had often been critical and expressed dissatisfaction with her work.

Eventually, however, Casey had to confront her supervisor, who told her not to make waves. It was only a few little changes, and she swore it would never happen again. She said that it would be pointless to bring it up now.

Things settled down for a while, but several months later Casey learned that her supervisor was once again fabricating information, doing things that would get her a bigger budget or buy her more time—and she again convinced Casey to keep her mouth shut. This went on for about a year, during which time two promotions were made within the company. My client applied for both but got neither. Her supervisor hadn't recommended her because she wanted to stay in control; she knew that she could manipulate Casey, so she kept her around.

Casey had become thoroughly dissatisfied with her job, resentful about her supervisor's lack of respect and integrity, and hopeless about receiving a promotion. She came into therapy to deal with the resulting depression, but she didn't realize that the first thing she had to deal with was all of the dishonoring. It was present in every aspect of this experience, and that's where the depression stemmed from.

The first thing Casey did wrong was allow her supervisor to disrespect her. Many people fall into this trap because they feel that they can't stand up to someone in authority, but as difficult as this may seem, it needs to be addressed. The energy of self-negation is heavy, and it carries with it serious consequences. Casey was miserable, she couldn't go forward in her company, and most important, she'd been willing to sacrifice her own integrity and self-respect because she was acting out of fear of being fired. She dishonored herself, the boss, her clients, and her business; and although it didn't seem so at first, she also dishonored the supervisor who was at the center of it all.

Once we discussed the Universal Laws and her energy, Casey knew what she had to do. She went in and told her supervisor that things would have to change. It was difficult, but she said that she needed more respect, and she knew that she deserved it. She also told her supervisor that the boss had to be told about the changed reports. She suggested that they go in to talk about it together, and to her surprise, the supervisor took her up on her offer.

Casey's honoring paid off. The boss appreciated her courage and her honesty, and he even forgave the supervisor who'd done all this, because she'd felt backed into a corner from having to supervise too many teams. In fact, the boss came up with an immediate solution: He made Casey a supervisor herself—with a promotion and salary to match—and he gave her some of the teams that her supervisor had been in charge of.

Things were made better for everyone. Casey was making more money and getting the recognition she longed for, and her supervisor was less stressed. The business was running more efficiently, and the boss was reassured that things were on the right track.

In this case, the question of honoring is clear, but there are many situations where the right decision is not so easy to find. You have to listen to your heart and look for the choice that resonates with your own sense of personal dignity. Right Action may not always be the easiest thing to do, but it's always the very best energy for everyone involved. When in doubt, refer to the following guidelines.

GUIDELINES FOR ENGAGING IN RIGHT ACTION

- Always take responsibility for yourself, your decisions, your emotions, your energy, and your behaviors.

- Make choices that promote your mental, physical, and emotional health. In every situation, ask what feels honoring to you.

- Seek genuine empowerment from within, not manipulation or control from without.

- Respect yourself and request that others do so also.

- Respect others, releasing judgment and living with compassion.

- Be truthful without being cruel.

- Always have the courage to live with dignity and self-actualization—no blame, no excuses.

When you're engaged in right action, you know it. Value sings in your heart and broadcasts your own beautiful melody in echoes of attraction. It triggers harmony and brings Universal right action back to you; it's the path of a genuinely loving intention.

Loving Intention

The primary intention behind right action is the creation of value and the expansion of love. In fact, love is the energetic catalyst to all successful creative manifestation. When we align our own thoughts with this vibrating force, we connect our frequency with the higher consciousness that created all things, and there's no greater power that we can enlist in the pursuit of our dreams.

The intention of love causes us to behave in ways that increase the value in our lives and the lives of others. When we talk about doing the "right" thing, we're making choices of reverence, value, and caring. In this way, we have the option to raise every vibration in every interaction and experience. We have the choice to accept instead of condemn, to support instead of discourage, to prioritize instead of dismiss, and to empower instead of control. Every day, we're faced with dozens of these kinds of choices—whether in the form of a passing compliment or a judgmental observation. The way you interact with others is a large part of what defines you—almost as much as the way you interact with yourself. When you choose to engage in respectful and honoring treatment, your energies vibrate with right action.

We're all special. Each of us, no matter what evidence we use to deny it, plays an extremely important part in the eternal scheme of things. So many people believe that our specialness is determined by grandiose acts, the accumulation of wealth, or the demonstration of extraordinary beauty or talent. But the workings of the Universe are like the workings of a huge, elaborate clock: There may be grand bells, beautiful moving characters, and gilded hands, but there are also countless pieces that have no outward appearance of importance. Yet even down to the smallest, seemingly most inconsequential part, each piece is important and special.

Our human structure is also a complicated network of many different functions, yet all are connected in some significant way. And whether we know it or not, each of us is a special part in the intricate mechanism of our Universe, bringing our unique energy to the grand experience.

If we choose to deny our own specialness and engage in deprecating our value or that of others, then we create a resistance in the smooth workings of the clock of our global purpose. If we learn to honor ourselves as special and to perceive all others—no matter what their circumstances—as valuable mechanisms in the Divine clockwork, then we're able to see the Universe as a whole, and our own reverence expands right action in all directions.

Right action isn't about morality; it's about energetic cause and effect. In fact, some people would call this the Law of Cause and Effect. Either way, the energetic truth is undeniable: You *will* get back the same energy that you put out toward others. If you're hateful and manipulative, eventually you'll see that same treatment in your life. If you're deceitful and dishonest, people will treat you that way after a while.

The Law of Magnetism says that your honoring should be focused on the treatment of yourself, while the Law of Right Action states that it should be focused on others. This may seem like a contradiction, but if you live in balance, you can prioritize others without sacrificing yourself, and you can make honoring—or right action—a part of your daily life.

The question of honoring is a subjective one, but the intention to do so is grounded in love. Your choice to engage in it will promote your sense of dignity and give you authentic—not fraudulent—power. You'll no longer need to gain your authority through the poisonous energies of arrogance or hostility—or even fear. Your ability to weigh the energetic consequences of your actions will go a long way in helping you do this, and when in doubt, reflect on the loving and honoring option. This is what right action is all about, and it's the choice that will always bring the *right* results.

AFFIRMATIONS FOR RIGHT ACTION

- *In all that I do and all that I think, I choose to honor myself always.*

- *More and more I am choosing to respect others and release judgment. I live with compassion.*

- *I understand that my own action comes back to me. I choose right action always.*

- *I release competition and choose to see people in a different light. Everyone is a blessing to me.*

- *I am beginning to be more conscious of the energy of others. From now on I choose love and acceptance in my attitude toward others.*

⊕ ⊕ ⊕

Chapter 7

THE LAW OF EXPANDING INFLUENCE

The Seventh Universal Law of Success

---

*"There is a thinking stuff from which all things
are made, and which, in its original state, permeates,
penetrates, and fills the interspaces of the universe."*

— W. D. Wattles

The seventh law reveals how your resonance influences others—
and how theirs has an effect you. All of life is an exchange of energy,
and it's always moving everywhere around us. An ongoing process of
accumulation creates the vibrational and emotional undercurrent to
all of our lives.

Of course, there are some quantum-physical phenomena that
demonstrate how this process works. The first influence is called *phase
entanglement.* In the natural world, particles converge and separate,
but often when two of them come together, they take a portion of the
other with them when they part. This is the essence of phase entanglement: When two entities meet, each one's energy becomes attached
to the other; each leaves something behind when it moves on.

The emotional experiences of humans can become phase entan-
gled, too. In fact, it happens every day to each one of us. We engage
with another person, and we take their vibration away with us—just as

they take ours with them. For example, when we argue with a moody teenager, we can become irritable ourselves. When we spend time with a depressed person, we may notice ourselves feeling down, even long after we've left them. And being around someone who's jubilant leaves us carrying that joy ourselves. Emotions are contagious, and each person's energy is influential.

This is a critically important principle in our pursuit of success. Because of the intricacies of energetic influence, we must be acutely aware of the relationships we forge, not only in our personal lives, but also in our social and professional lives as well. The spirit of others not only influences our thoughts, moods, and sense of well-being, it shapes our choices as well.

You can see how this pattern would be an important consideration in owning or managing a business—the phenomenon makes it especially important to hire people of integrity. Since energetic influences expand in the world, you wouldn't want someone of lower vibrations spreading the energies of neglect and deceit in your workplace. For the same reason, it's also important for *you* to have integrity in your business dealings.

There's an old adage that says, "As the King, so goes the country." This means that the resonant attitudes and actions of the leader are picked up by his people and spread far and wide. It's a truth that we can still see working in the world today. This is the case for countries, as well as communities, companies, and families.

⚖ The **Law of Expanding Influence** shows that your own energy expands in the world and has influence in your personal arena and in the world at large. You can—and do—have an impact on everything from the productivity of your company and the harmony of your family all the way to the peace of the world! The power of your own personal vibration becomes global by virtue of this law. When you choose to live with reverence in your heart and direct it toward those around you, that positive energy spreads to all your circles of influence . . . and eventually, your intention for harmony expands in the consciousness of every human being.

If you want your family life to be more peaceful, *you* must create that intention within yourself first. If you want your workers to be more industrious, *you* must begin to project that energy in your own life. Everyone needs to understand the influence and extent of their own power. In the pursuit of success, the requirements are honesty, enthusiasm, encouragement, and support. Whether we're talking about a well-oiled business or a happy and loving relationship, these are the personal wavelengths that are necessary to produce the most desirable results.

Expanding Action

As we saw earlier, Bell's theorem of nonlocality reveals that what happens in one location can have a significant influence in a far-off, distant place. This is true for your personal energy and action, too. In this amazing Universe of ours, anything can happen anyplace, anytime. Because of the quantum connections we all share, our actions and intentions can bring immediate results from surprising people and unexpected locales. From the tiniest particle to the greatest mass, the Universe is a vibrating realm of potential, an abundant field of all possibilities. Because of these vast opportunities and our nonlocal power, we should remain encouraged to always continue to take action in the direction of our goals. The results may not come in the manner we expect, but with the right energy, those results will come just the same.

A friend of mine experienced this phenomenon when she was attempting to adopt a baby. She was going through a domestic adoption with an agency that found prospective birth mothers, each of whom had the choice of several couples with which to place her baby.

After nearly a year of trying to find someone through her agency, Megan was ready to give up. Her lawyer suggested that she send letters to the obstetricians and gynecologists in the area, because they often had patients who had an unwanted pregnancy and were looking to place their child in an adoptive home. So she sent out hundreds of letters and attended many meetings, still with no luck.

During this time, she often called me to express her frustration, and I advised her to keep taking action in every direction. Whenever you plant the seeds of intention, you never know when or where they're going to bloom. She continued her activities in every way she could, and several months later she got a call from the original agency that she'd long ago given up on. They had a birth mother who was due the following January and had picked out Megan and her husband, Sam, as one of three prospective adoptive families.

Megan and Sam would now have to go through several interviews with the birth parents to determine if they'd be chosen. She was going to give up on sending the letters and making other contacts, but I advised her not to. I told her that continuing to work on the situation in many different ways would help her reach her goal.

Expanded actions—that is, looking in every direction—help reduce urgency, keeping away the negative influences of paradoxical intent. Megan experienced this, because the more she kept working on her other options, the less desperate she felt about being chosen. She'd already had several potential adoptions fall through, and she needed to surrender her attachment to this outcome in order to attract the ultimate results. All her activity helped her to remember that what she wanted was a baby—not necessarily *this* one. By continuing to see options in all sorts of different directions, she was able to let go of the urgency and obsession that might have sabotaged her results.

> ⚛ In addition to reducing urgency, continued action greatly expands intention. The more you undertake, the more energy you send out regarding your intention. Each and every deed is like placing another order with the Universe, and you never know how or when it's going to respond. You may plant the seeds in one area but end up seeing the results somewhere else entirely.

That's what happened to Megan. She'd given up hope on the agency, but all her other actions brought them back to her. Then, while she was going through the interviews with the birth parents, she continued working in all sorts of other directions. It not only kept her calm, but it also reaffirmed her intention to make this dream a reality.

In the long run, all her efforts paid off. Slowly but surely, the other potential couples were weeded out, and Megan and Sam were chosen to be the adoptive parents of this birth mother's little boy to come. Her dream became a reality—all because she refused to stop taking action.

The energetic power of our nonlocal nature is profoundly effective. *Every thought and every deed plants a new seed in the garden of our destiny.* We may not be immediately aware of the effects, but it's important to know that the process of intention and influence has no end. It always brings results in one way or another, so we might as well intend the best and take positive action in every direction. In this way, we open ourselves to *all* the options that the Universe may have in store—even the unexpected ones.

JOURNAL FOR SUCCESS

Use your journal to explore how you can expand your personal intentions in even more directions. Considering each specific goal or desire, investigate some different—or perhaps even unorthodox—ways to work on making them a reality. If necessary, do some research or ask friends to help you brainstorm ideas. Jot them down and add new ones whenever they may come up. Once you have some fresh approaches in mind, don't be afraid to implement them. Sometimes the best results can come from the most unusual concepts.

Expanding Worldwide

The ripples of our influence aren't limited to the pursuit of our own personal goals. In fact, this is just a small part of consciousness creation. Whether we realize it or not, our impact expands outward to reach even the far corners of the world. The seventh Universal Law shows that your own energy moves out to bond with other energies that are similar. These clouds of bonded vibrations become fields of consciousness that exude immeasurable influence on the experience of our species.

These worldwide fields of consciousness are called morphogenetic fields, or M-fields for short. Like the electromagnetic and gravitational fields, M-fields are forces that are capable of swaying the very nature of our lives. Emotion and information are the energies that build in those fields, affecting the significant transitions of our species. These great storehouses of shared consciousness are fed by each and every individual's energy—including yours—and then that accumulated power billows out and touches others.

There are two major fields of emotional consciousness, that of love and that of fear or hate. As individuals, all our thoughts, beliefs, choices, and behaviors contribute to the expansion of one or the other of these. Every time that we make a loving choice, whether it's for ourselves or someone else, we feed the field of love. But every time we engage in hate or judgment—again whether it's directed inward or outward—we're feeding the field of fear.

As the accumulated energy builds in each of these realms, the resonance of that particular energy increases in the Universe, and the consciousness of love or hate moves out to influence the choices and experiences of others. Whatever is fed the most will have the greatest power in our world.

This is our individual responsibility: to choose love in our own minds and lives, and in the lives of others, thereby accelerating the energy of caring in the world. If we don't, then hate and fear will accelerate instead. This isn't a function of the fields having any specific intention, because they're actually impartial. Just as gravity has no emotional investment in the literal ups and downs of our activities, the fields of love and hate are indifferent to how we deal with their influence in the world.

Each person's intention determines the course of humanity; every individual's emotions and actions feed the energy and power that you see all around. So if you want love—rather than hate—to expand in your relationships, business, and world, then you must engage in more caring energy toward yourself and others. As you'll see in the next chapter, the power of love is always at your disposal. Bring it to your consciousness, energy, and intention, and you'll not only bring blessings to your own life, your expanding influence will bring them to the entire world.

AFFIRMATIONS FOR MY EXPANDING INFLUENCE

- *I know that my energy expands in the world. The more action I take toward my goals, the more my intention is embraced by the Universe.*

- *I walk and move at a comfortable pace. I do everything at a leisurely tempo. I am relaxed, and I carry that calm and tranquil energy to others.*

- *I know that my own energy expands in my life and in the Universe. I choose unconflicted energy now. With every peaceful thought I think, the power of peace expands.*

- *I look for the joy I can bring to others. It is a gift to myself to be of service.*

- *I see the value in everyone around me. Together we share the energy of the world.*

⊕   ⊕   ⊕

PART II

THE SIX PERSONAL POWERS OF SUCCESS

The Universal Laws place the responsibility of success squarely upon your shoulders. To make your dreams a reality, you'll have to investigate what it will take to put those powerful forces into play for you. The demands of the laws may involve changing the way that you do things—and how you think about them—not because of mere idealism, but because of the fundamental nature of your own vibrating essence.

People often long for change but do very little to actively bring it about. They look at it as some future occurrence, thinking things such as, *When my prospects or finances change—then everything will be okay.* But this is a passive approach to an active expectation, and it's not likely to yield very beneficial results. Instead of waiting, you need to make it happen!

Transformation isn't a future event; it's the present activity that stimulates what's to come. Change is not the goal, it's the consistent process that leads to your desire. The quality of your life is up to you, and if you're not happy with what's going on now, then you need to make new choices in the present in order to ensure a better tomorrow. In this way, you *do* have the ability to magnetize success!

In fact, all the resources you'll ever need already exist within you. There are six truly dynamic personal powers that are a part of your nature and always available. You can utilize them in a conscious way to change everything you attract to your life, because ultimately, success comes from taking control. When you start to use your innate and often-neglected gifts, your life will take an entirely new direction.

Each of these power requires an awareness on your part, and some may demand significant changes, but don't resist. Remember the old adage: *If you change nothing, nothing will change.*

◈　◈　◈

Chapter 8

THE POWER
OF LETTING GO

The First Personal Power of Success

---

*"Progress is impossible without change, and those who
cannot change their minds cannot change anything."*

— George Bernard Shaw

Letting go is the first personal power because it's the necessary first step to change. Creating a wonderful destiny is like creating a garden: It's pointless to plant the seeds of beautiful blossoms if your plot is overgrown with weeds. You must remove those unwanted plants, or they'll choke out the new flowers before they even bloom. The same is true for the seeds of your success: In order to produce the creative consciousness and magnetic energies that will harvest the results you desire, it's important to dig up—and let go of—the unhealthy patterns of the past. This is a key requirement for changing your energy and shifting your consciousness. If you want real success, it's very likely that some of your old patterns won't work for you any longer.

There are several levels of letting go, with the first and most obvious being physical. In this chapter, you'll also learn about mental, emotional, and behavioral release, as well as how to let go of attachments.

Physical Release

Engaging in exercise or other types of movement on a regular basis is important for clearing out old energy and creating a new, lighter, and more attractive vibration. This is helpful for many reasons. First, it releases any emotional trauma or unhappy memories that may be trapped in your cells and body. Physical activity and deep breathing help shift that stuck energy and move it out of your personal resonance.

In addition, regular exercise assists you in releasing the chronic tension in your life. Stress is a very unhealthy and unattractive energy, and over time, it will draw even more tense situations and uptight people to you. The most attractive vibration you can project is that of a relaxed, peaceful, and confident spirit.

To relax your body, make sure that you breathe deeply and get regular muscle movement. Stretching and massage will also help, but you'll need to relax your mind and emotions, too. The process of mental release starts with letting go of your old negative thoughts, but it has a significant impact on your physical and emotional vibrations as well, since your entire being is interconnected.

Mental Release

Our minds generate energy constantly, sending out signals that convey our deepest beliefs and most common thoughts. Everything we do and think has an immediate energetic consequence, although it may take a while to manifest in the physical world. *Your persistent thoughts—whether they're good or bad—create the greatest consequences of your life, whether you want them to or not.*

As you learned in the last chapter, your thoughts are a doubly powerful force, since they're the source of both your mental and emotional energy. Negative self-talk creates difficult emotions such as depression and fear, which are very damaging to your personal energy field. These kinds of conclusions must be released if you want to create a resonance of success.

So many people go through their days—even their entire lives—simply reacting, without any conscious awareness of what their thoughts are or what effects they may be having. But to change your energy and your consciousness, you need to be aware of the clues of negative thinking.

The biggest hint is in your emotions. Whenever you're having an uncomfortable feeling, there's almost always a negative thought behind it. So when you catch yourself feeling fear, depression, guilt, embarrassment, or even just nervousness, ask yourself, *What am I thinking?* Look deep inside to find the negative conclusion that's making you so upset. You have the power to change your energy by letting go of your old thought patterns, but to do so you need information.

Two of the most common negative thought patterns are judgment and worry. They're important to know, because without identifying the source of your negative energy, it will be impossible to change it. You must figure out and release the toxic beliefs that plague you the most. Remember that your life moves in the direction of your dominant thought, and that this truth is energetically irresistible. If your primary opinions are negative, then you must choose to let them go, or your life will never move in a more positive direction.

JUDGMENT

Judgment is one of the two most common negative thought patterns. It comes in three major forms—judging yourself, others, and experiences—all of which are poisonous to the energy that you project.

Consistent self-criticism broadcasts signals of low self-esteem, a frequency that's guaranteed to bring rejection from the outside world. Also, the Law of Right Action clearly indicates that your judgment of others is bound to return, sending out a hostile energy that throws up obstacles to your pursuit of successful connections. In addition, that hateful influence expands in the world, not only bringing more misery to yourself, but also to others.

Finally, when you're judgmental about your life experiences, you find yourself enjoying less and less of your personal activities, until nothing seems to be good enough or special enough to make you happy. This becomes a deep pool of dissatisfaction, drowning any joyful energy that you could be projecting, resisting any joy you could attract.

You can release this toxic pattern by investigating the common negative statements from each type of judgment listed here. Place a check mark next to the ones that most represent your kind of thinking—and be honest!

1. **Judgment of Self**

   _____ I'm too inexperienced (uneducated, poor, etc.) to succeed.

   _____ I'm a failure; I'll always be a failure.

   _____ I never do anything right. What's wrong with me?

   _____ It's just my luck! I'm such a loser.

   _____ I'm getting so old (ugly, fat, slow, etc.).

   _____ I feel so stupid (incompetent, incapable, etc.).

2. **Judgment of Others**

   _____ What a jerk!

   _____ He's so stupid (lazy, weak, etc.); he doesn't deserve that promotion.

   _____ He never does anything right.

   _____ I can't believe that she's wearing that old thing. How embarrassing!

   _____ She's getting so old (ugly, fat, slow, etc.).

   _____ Those idiot liberals (conservatives, Democrats, Republicans, blacks, whites, Hispanics, etc.)! They don't know what they're talking about.

3. **Judgment of Experience**

   _____ This movie is terrible; what a waste of time.

   _____ I can't stand this place (this weather, this person, etc.).

   _____ My job is going nowhere.

   _____ This party is so boring.

   _____ This situation is lousy. Nothing good is going to come from this.

   _____ I hate doing housework (yard work, paperwork, etc.).

WORRY

The second major type of negative thought pattern is worry. You can fret about the future, what people think, and even the past. While it's not uncommon to be concerned about what lies ahead, you have to ask yourself: *What good does this really do?* It only creates an energy of anxiety that moves out into the world in clouds of agitation, creating the negative future that you were stressed about.

People-pleasing is another pointless mental activity. Striving to gain the approval of others only means that you don't believe in yourself, and that resonance is a compelling obstacle to success.

Finally, brooding about the past is as counterproductive as fearing the future, because it utterly destroys the energy of the present. It's time to let go of the worry and take your power back. Drop the analysis and start to engage in trust.

Place a check mark next to the following statements that tend to represent your mode of thinking. All of these are ways that you agitate your energy, and they have to stop if you really want to succeed.

1. **Worry "What-Ifs"**

   _____What if I don't get that job?

   _____What if I fail?

   _____What if he doesn't like me?

   _____What if I don't say (do, wear, etc.) the right thing?

   _____What if I get hurt or sick?

   _____What if I don't get a good evaluation? What if I get fired?

2. **Worrying about What People Think**

   _____He's never going to like me. I know he won't ask me out.

   _____She must think I'm a jerk.

   _____They don't think I can do this job.

   _____My boss must think I'm a real screwup. I can tell he hates me.

   _____If I take a second serving, they're going to think I'm a pig.

   _____If I don't do what they want, then they won't like me.

3. Brooding and Overanalysis

_____ I can't believe I said that!

_____ If only I'd done something different, then everything would be okay.

_____ I wonder what I can do to mend things. I have to fix this!

_____ Why does this always happen to me? Why couldn't it have turned out differently?

_____ I still remember how badly I was treated. I don't know if I'll ever get over it!

_____ Why did I make that decision? What a mistake that was!

What kind of thinking did you check the most? Do you tend to judge yourself or others? Perhaps you're a worrier, speculating about the future, wondering what people think, or overanalyzing everything, or maybe you've marked statements in each category. Whatever pattern you identify with the most, you have to work on letting it go.

JOURNAL FOR SUCCESS

In your journal, write down each of the previously checked thoughts, and then replace it with a more positive and optimistic conclusion. For example, replace *What if don't get the job?* with *What if I do get the job?!* or *If I don't get this position, another one will come along. I'll be fine.* You don't have to be convinced of the truth of your new statements at first, but you *must* write down your options in order to initiate this important change.

While you continue to work out these cognitive patterns, notice any other negative thoughts that may come up and write them in your journal. Make sure that you also write a replacement statement for each one. Continue this process until you've seen some real changes—in your mental activity, your emotions, and what you attract.

As you're engaged in this transition, be careful not to be too harsh on yourself for your worry or judgment. After all, that's just adding more of the energy that you're trying to let go! Instead of condemning yourself for your negative thinking, simply forgive yourself and reaffirm your intention to move on. Don't make yourself crazy over it; just make it a gentle, peaceful determination. In time, your strong new attitude will become a way of life.

You see, there's absolutely no room for worry or judgment in the intention to create success. You must let go of those reactions and choose other options that project a more positive and dynamic energy. No matter how difficult it may seem, make sure that you *keep letting go* of the old negativity and open yourself up to a new optimism in your thinking.

Releasing your negative thoughts is a requirement of the Universal Laws and one of the most valuable tools for changing your destiny. Remember that your thoughts, emotions, and beliefs are the most significant source of your energy. Every single idea moves outward from you in waves of resonant information.

If you believe that you can't succeed, then that experience must be what your consciousness creates. You simply can't afford to repeat your negative thoughts any longer. Let them go and choose to speak a new language to yourself and others. This will create much more positive emotions, which are the most powerful energy accelerators to truly boundless success.

Emotional Release

Feelings represent a strong vibration, and they carry very clear messages with them. Whether you realize it or not, if you haven't ventilated your feelings, you could still be sending out old signals of grief, anger, rejection, and other negative emotions that are lingering in your energy field.

Many people have a difficult time expressing or even identifying their feelings. They often experience trauma and disappointment without ever giving voice to the emotions involved, accumulating clouds of negative energy that broadcast abrasive resonance in every direction. You carry these with you like "Pigpen" in the *Peanuts* cartoons, walking through life with billows of dark vibration hanging all around. People feel that energy and are repulsed.

To get rid of that black fog, you need to let go of unexpressed feelings from the past. It's similar to cleaning the junk out of your house so that you can make room for the beautiful new things in your life. In fact, it may be necessary to purge your old feelings even if the difficult events happened quite a while ago. If you've never had the opportunity to release them, the emotions from distant experiences may be creating some powerful signals in your energy field, blocking new achievements and sending out painful signals.

This isn't to say that you have to go back and relive every trauma or difficult passage. You know which difficulties still may be haunting you, so get out your journal and start writing about it. Express all the feelings that you still need to release; don't obsess about it, just ventilate it.

Be especially conscious of the assumptions that you made about your upsetting experiences. At the end of each journal entry ask yourself, *What conclusions did I draw from this experience that I may want to change now?* Write down any negative thoughts or beliefs, then replace them with new ones.

For example, if you got fired and experienced emotions such as anger, fear, and rejection, you may have concluded, *I'll never be accepted. I'll never be a success.* Turn that thought around by ventilating the feelings and then writing down a healthy belief, such as *I'm still capable of succeeding. I deserve to believe in myself, and I choose to do so now.* Continue letting go of both the negative thoughts and difficult emotions from the past in this way, always affirming your present capabilities and your expectations of a bright and happy future.

In addition to releasing the feelings of days gone by, it's also important to let go of them as they come up. You can use your journal for this, also. While it doesn't have to be a daily activity, if you do this on a regular basis, you'll find that it's easier to change your thinking and your vibrations as well. Holding on to negative emotions such as resentment, anger, or fear blocks your energy and significantly impacts your results. Relinquish them, and your energy will be clear, open, and ready to receive.

Behavioral Release

Letting go of unhealthy and harmful behaviors, especially indulgences and addictions, is also important in creating an attractive energy and productive consciousness. People indulge in all sorts of things, including alcohol, drugs, cigarettes, food, television, exercise, gossip, sex, work, relationships, and drama. We turn to them to provide us with a sense of distraction or escape. When we have that drink, eat too much, or take a drug, it helps numb our emotions and makes us feel better, at least for a little while. When we turn on the television, we zone out; when we eat the chips or cookies, we believe that we're comforting ourselves in some way.

Even things such as manipulation, deceit, or meanness are compelling, because they can make us feel better at the time—but this is false comfort. Eventually, our harmful behaviors only make us feel worse, and they may in time turn into the even more toxic behaviors of addiction.

When you engage in any of these actions, what are you running away from? What pain are you trying to numb yourself to? At its deepest level, it's an emptiness that comes from forgetting who you really are—your higher, grander identity, your connection to the Divine and your inherent value there. Whether you're aware of it or not, this seemingly lost link is the real source of your unrest.

But the light of your Divine identity is always there, and the power that you seek from outside is alive within. No matter what you've been told, your value is a shining vibration that's always intrinsic to your being, right down to your very cells. Whatever difficult experience or painful treatment may have compelled you to escape into unhealthy patterns, it's now time to deal with that, to express your feelings, figure out the negative conclusions, and move on to new, more healthy and truthful ones.

It's time to fill the void you feel with the light of your own sacred identity. This is all the refuge you'll ever need—and the real solution to all that you seek. Behaviors of escapism, indulgence, and addiction only create an even bigger hole, taking you further and further away from your real source of comfort and power. Moreover, they destroy your energy with vibrations of need, fear, and overindulgence, driving you deeper into desperation and attracting more and more unpleasant results.

While it's difficult to rid yourself of these habits, you can practice intervening on the behaviors for just ten minutes at a time. Create a system of replacement activities and write them in your journal. Enlist the support of someone you trust; even get professional help if you need it, because this is too important to dismiss.

When you engage in an indulgent or harmful action, remind yourself of the energetic truth that *all* your choices create your energy. Do you really want the vibration of escapism to be what you project? If the answer is no, then consistently make the choice to let the habit go.

Again, be careful not to judge yourself for falling into old, unhealthy patterns, because doing so only adds fuel to the negative fire—which actually increases your need to escape. So as you're letting go of everything else, release the judgment for failing to let go.

⚛ Learning to release is a lifelong process. Every day, renew your determination to let go of the past and relinquish the worry. This will clear the way for your new, healthy choices that are certain to make your life sparkle. When you give up the thoughts, emotions, and behaviors that have been holding you back, you'll open up your vital energy and resonate a brilliant and beautiful vibration for all the world to see.

Letting Go of Attachment

The last important thing to release is attachment. When we look around, we can see all sorts of things that we may feel attached to—the pictures on the walls, the jewelry on our neck and hands, the furniture in the room, and the car in the driveway are all things that we take pride in owning. But the price of possession is attachment, and it's very easy to become *too* invested in having "stuff." In very subtle ways, this sends out a needy, hoarding type of energy, and the more stuff we have, the more it seems that we need.

I'm not saying that we should never want material things, we just need to be mindful of our attachment to them. I'm talking about thoughts such as *I need this to be happy, I need this car and this jewelry, and I need these things around me to be content.* These are very dangerous ideas in two important ways.

First, they encourage the belief that material things have the power to make us happy. Unfortunately, whenever we think that something outside of us can bring us joy, we give away our power to do that for ourselves. We also set a precedent that keeps us striving—moving us dangerously close to the energy of desperation. As we need to acquire even more, we find ourselves struggling in an unending effort to keep up.

Believing that things are the key to joy also puts us in a very precarious situation. After all, what happens if we should lose our acquisitions? It's an ever-present possibility that sets us up for ceaseless worry. We live with an undercurrent of fear that's always pushing us to seek reassurance, and we're continually worried about potential loss.

A RELEASING-ATTACHMENT EXERCISE

In order to let go of attachment, take a look at the things around you. Survey your various material goods, take a deep breath, and affirm: *I like that, but I do not need it to be happy.* Look at your jewelry, your furniture, your car, and even your home; and say it to each item in turn. This may feel very scary at first, but in many ways it's actually quite liberating. In time, it will create a peacefulness inside that transcends acquisitions. You'll recognize that happiness comes from your own peace of mind, not from your stuff.

Let yourself do this every day, applying the process to the things you own and the choices you make. You'll be amazed by the feeling of freedom it creates, and it will purify your energy, too. In addition, the magic of letting go gets wonderful things back. Practice the art of surrendering by giving away something that you value. Bestow it on someone else with grace, generosity, and complete release. Doing these exercises will be a big help in engaging the Laws of Desire and Paradoxical Intent. Remember, the paradox is that when you release your attachment, you gain everything.

AFFIRMATIONS FOR LETTING GO

- *I am becoming more and more comfortable with letting go. I let go of the past and all my fears. I am free.*

- *I release any negative thought that may come up. I choose a better energy now.*

- *I let go of unhealthy and dishonoring habits. I now create a healthy new lifestyle.*

- *I let go of attachment. I know that it is really my attitude that brings me happiness—and nothing else.*

- *I embrace a peaceful attitude. I let go of worry, hurry, and the need for control.*

⊕　⊕　⊕

Chapter 9

THE POWER OF CONSCIOUSNESS

The Second Personal Power of Success

---

*"Consciousness is the creative element in the universe.
Without it, nothing would appear."*

— Fred Alan Wolf, Ph.D.

Not too long ago, the words *physics* and *consciousness* were considered mutually exclusive. One was strict science, and the other was merely an abstract concept relegated to the fields of psychology or philosophy. Now scientists all over the world are studying the physics of consciousness, and it's widely accepted that it does indeed create reality.

Physics is the science of possibilities, and the power of consciousness is the source. But what is the process of manifestation? How do things come to be in the world? More important, how are our personal destinies shaped by our own consciousness?

Through quantum physics, we know that reality isn't separate from the observation of it, and the same is true for our own lives. What we experience in the real world can't be separated from our perception of it. In fact, the study of biomechanics reveals that the brain isn't even capable of distinguishing the difference between reality and memory.

The exact same neurons are sparked when we see something as when we merely remember it.

> ❄ The key to consciousness creation is found in your perception—what you perceive about yourself and your reality, and how it makes you feel. In fact, this creates many of the chemical and emotional responses of your body and your mind. It's an ongoing process of cause and effect: Perception stimulates reaction; reaction reinforces perception. Your consciousness is so powerful that it not only determines the emotional quality of your life, it evokes significant physiological responses as well.

The process begins when a single emotion or thought triggers the hypothalamus gland in the brain to release certain peptides. These substances move out to receptors where they dock in the cells, creating a chemical reaction that matches and perpetuates the original emotional state. Whether positive or negative, similar thoughts will produce similar peptides and similar emotions.

In time, the repetition of this pattern will shut down other receptors that could be available to the peptides of differing emotional states. In this way, your perception becomes fixed, repeatedly setting off a biochemical chain of events that perpetuates the same old feelings. This is how emotional habits—and even addictions—are formed. It may sound complicated, but it's a relatively simple and very spontaneous process. And it has a huge impact on consciousness and energy production because of the extensive cognitive, emotional, and biochemical involvement.

Let's look at an example of how the process might work: You pass a certain building in your neighborhood many times, with no emotional or cognitive reaction; you just observe it being there. One day, just at a time in your life when you're starting to look for a job, you walk by and see a sign out front announcing an opening and giving a phone number. You experience excitement, and your hypothalamus releases peptides that match and perpetuate that feeling, as you go home, call the number, and set up the interview. And every day when you pass the building—*or even just when you think about it*—you have the same biochemical reaction, and you get excited. You're hired, and for the first several months your reaction remains the same.

Over time, however, you slowly but surely begin to experience the job in a different way. Perhaps a certain person or task causes unhappiness, and you now start to have a negative perception, which produces peptides matching that feeling. Even when you're just getting ready for work or thinking about it, the unpleasant perception stimulates the neuropeptides that match and perpetuate that emotion.

This goes on for years, until you hear about a new job opening up on the other side of town. You apply for it and get it, and you start to produce the peptides that match that excited feeling again. This new position continues to stimulate those upbeat emotions, but it only lasts a couple of years, until the company moves to Mexico.

Now you're out of work, and the need for money changes your perception once more. You start to look at the old place as not being so bad. Every time you pass that building—in fact, every time you think of it—you wish that you were back there. It may have had its problems, but it's certainly preferable to no job at all. In every memory and longing, your thoughts, emotions, and physiological and chemical reactions create a consciousness of loss and regret, which then becomes your filter of manifestation. It's a circle of situation and creation. Your experience creates the emotions that perpetuate the experience.

While it seems as if this process is just a natural sequence of thought and feeling, it's important to know that the chemistry is a major reason why you tend to stay so stuck in your mental and emotional patterns. It takes a conscious intention to turn your conclusions and perceptions around in order to get out of this biochemical self-sabotage. The chemistry that matches and perpetuates your emotional responses is a significant factor in your energy projection, and your consciousness is the key to both this internal biological source and your external life consequences.

There are two very specific steps that you can take to change your patterns of negative perception and the resulting neuropeptide involvement:

- When you feel a negative emotion welling up within, stop and take a deep breath. Affirm: *My body is releasing neuro-peptides of peace and tranquility. A gentle wave of serenity and relaxation is moving through me now.*

- When you see or experience something that ignites a negative reaction, affirm: *I can let that go. I release and relax. I choose peace.*

When you choose to engage in more positive cognitions, you produce the neuropeptides that match hope, excitement, and happiness. This changes your mind, emotions, and body, right down to your chemical reactions; and as a result, the energy of your awareness will change as well. In this way, your consciousness is the strongest force of your destiny creation.

Consciousness PIE

There are three main ingredients that activate your power of consciousness: **p**erception, **i**magination, and **e**xpectation, or what I refer to as consciousness PIE. A positive experience in these mental and emotional elements of your life is absolutely necessary in your pursuit of success. In fact, whether positive or not, these are the three key pieces of consciousness creation. They're energetically linked together in a dynamic process that can actually give you an amazing amount of control over the consequences of your life. Let's take a look at how each piece works.

THE POWER OF PERCEPTION

You've already seen that your perception stimulates the production of neuropeptides that perpetuate emotional experiences. When you see something as being negative, it produces a biochemical reaction that reinforces the unfavorable emotional state, and the opposite is true as well. This alone should be motivation enough to keep working on consciously creating a positive outlook, but let's also examine how perception affects energy.

The way you see things is filtered through your history, yet it's powerful enough to create your future. In very real ways, this is what defines you, right down to your physiological reality. How you perceive yourself, your world, and your future is the cognitive foundation under-lying all your moods. Studies show that self-perception and self-talk impact serotonin and endorphin levels, which perpetuate ongoing feelings such as depression or joy.

But this piece of the consciousness PIE is so powerful that its influ-ence doesn't stop there. There are documented cases where people with multiple personality disorder manifest varying diagnosable physical conditions when a different personality is "in control." Conditions such as diabetes and vision problems become physiological issues when a particular identity takes over. Even though the same body may have no such problem at other times, when it exists in the perception of the controlling personality, then it becomes a very real physical challenge.

This isn't the only case where consciousness changes physiology. People are able to walk on burning hot coals without injury by shifting their perception, and I myself experienced this phenomenon many years ago. I took a fire-walking class in which nearly 100 people were taught how to change their state of mind by completely shifting their focus from the experience of stepping on hot coals to the memory of something that evoked thrilling and happy sensations.

I envisioned myself skiing down my favorite slope in Colorado, visu-ally and emotionally putting myself on that ski run in the crisp, cold, beautiful mountains. This changed my neuropeptides and physiology, and I was able to walk over 15 feet of burning-hot coals that were at a temperature of several hundred degrees.

I was completely uninjured, but there *were* some people who burned themselves, because they were too locked into the framework of their expectations. They saw the burning coals to be a danger, so they experienced them that way. But those of us who changed our perception were able to completely transform our physical reality.

You, too, have the power to alter your environment. No matter what's happened to you, you don't have to perceive the world in the same old way. Instead, you can use your power of letting go to release your old, limited outlook. *No matter what you may be experiencing, remember that you always have the option to choose a new perception.*

This is the key to consciousness-created reality: What you observe to be true frames your awareness. Instead of staying stuck in your past view of things, you can now approach your life as a blank canvas. You can create a new picture, see things differently, and imagine everything around you in an entirely new way. In fact, this is the next important piece of your consciousness PIE.

IMAGERY IS EVERYTHING

As you make positive shifts in your perceptions, you'll find it easier and easier to fire up your imagination. I'm not just speaking about your ability to daydream and fantasize about your future; I'm referring to your ability to actually create mental images—living pictures of what you want your future to look like. This is a powerful skill when pursuing specific scenarios of success.

Where processing mental imagery is concerned, the brain can't distinguish between present events and past memories. Nor can it tell the difference between what's vividly imagined and what's real. In fact, a number of physicists don't even believe that a single reality exists. The Many-Worlds Interpretation (MWI) suggests that several realities are going on all at the same time, and there are some scientists who believe that you can choose the one you want. This may sound like science fiction, but it only goes to show the unlimited possibilities of your life. You need to *imagine* all that you can experience! Don't limit yourself—to create it you must see it.

    ❧   Your ability to imagine vivid pictures of success will establish that reality in your energy and consciousness first. The images that you see in your mind will then become the what you see in your life. If the pictures floating in your imagination right now don't correspond with what you truly want to experience in your future, you need to develop some new ones. To create success, you must create successful images.

Consciousness-created imaging happens on two levels. Perform the following steps often to establish a powerful new perception of success.

1. Successful self-imaging: You need to paint the pictures of how you want yourself to be, look, feel, and act. Create a vivid image of the total package just as you desire it, and then hold it close in your mind. Move within it, live it, feel it, and believe it. Let yourself envision and experience it many times a day, and before long, you'll become it!

2. Successful imaging of your specific goals: Create clear, bright pictures of exactly what it is that you want. Make the imagery so vivid that you feel as if you're already there in the center of it. Imagine the joyous outcome of each goal, and then put the mental photograph of that *future* event into your *memory*. See it as a favorite moment already captured in a photo album, one that you turn to over and over again. In this way, you're informing your brain that that image of the future has already happened; that reality exists. Turn back to this often, whenever you need to motivate yourself or create a clear consciousness of your goal.

Once you've established your successful pictures clearly, you must focus *only* on those images. You must let go of any thought that negates or diminishes them in any way. When you visualize each one, enlarge it. See it clearly, not off in the distance or moving left or right, since that could change the power of its reality, as well as its energetic timing. Hold the image in the center of your mind, so close that it's all that you can see. Make it real and it will become so.

The more carefully you inspect and experience your images of joyous outcomes, the more your brain and consciousness will accept them as reality. As you continue to reproduce each picture—clear, close, and centered in your thinking—you'll create more and more of the positive emotions that charge a highly creative consciousness and magnetic energy. This will help fine-tune your expectation, the final piece of your consciousness PIE.

EXPECT THE BEST

It's useless to create the image of success if that reality is beyond your comprehension. There's a big difference between what you desire and what you expect, so it's important to consciously and constantly anticipate the best. To facilitate that, you need to find out what your hidden expectations are.

You tend to look at each day with certain assumptions, so it's only natural to project your "normal" patterns into the future. The problem is that if you're often dissatisfied with the present, it's pretty hard to create positive expectations about the future.

Underneath it all, how do you look at your daily life? Do you hope for acceptance, yet expect rejection? Do you long for success, yet anticipate failure? Do you wish for happiness, yet resign yourself to boredom, drudgery, or disappointment? If you expect today to be difficult and unsuccessful, then you'll only look forward to more of the same. But you can choose to create new expectations and beliefs about what you're capable of achieving—today, tomorrow, and always.

In the battle between desire and expectation, the Universe is far more likely to give you what you expect. Why is this the case? Your desires are where your *wishes* are; your expectations are where your *beliefs* are, and in the formula of destiny creation, nothing is more powerful than your beliefs.

Your convictions must support a positive expectation—the fundamental assumption of a valuable outcome. You can no longer continue to desire the best and expect the worst, because the Universe simply can't reconcile such a split of consciousness. You must begin to look for the best in both your day-to-day life and in the fulfillment of your dreams, knowing that you're capable of bringing your highest and happiest awareness to all that you experience. Take your power back and create a conscious perception of your ideal day and your ideal future. Understand what it looks and feels like and that you're capable of making it happen.

Your daily expectations also accelerate your energetic momentum, so you must make your everyday view the same as your vision of the future. If you want to be a success, you can no longer pigeonhole, limit, or dismiss your desires. Instead, you need to move them out into a grander view. Unlimited expectations will yield boundless results when they're a part of the entire recipe for successful consciousness creation:

- Positive perception
- Vivid and creative imagination
- Excitedly optimistic expectation

Even just a small shift in any one of these attitudes can create a major change in your reality, because consciousness is one of your greatest powers. It's the steadfast choice to live in an awakened state in the here-and-now, one in which you freely choose a new perception, view, and expectation of what is—and what can be—real for you. Choose it now!

AFFIRMATIONS FOR A POWER CONSCIOUSNESS

- *I choose a strong, successful perception of myself. I am capable and deserving.*

- *I visualize myself just as I would like to be. I see myself as confident, vibrant, and happy—now and always.*

- *I expect the best. In my daily life and in my future, I always anticipate excellence.*

- *I live in an aware and conscious state. I consciously choose the thoughts and images that create a great reality.*

- *I visualize my goals with excitement and belief. I receive many wonderful blessings in my life.*

⊕　⊕　⊕

Chapter 10

THE POWER OF ENERGY

The Third Personal Power of Success

---

*"The world is a looking-glass, and gives back
to every man the reflection of his own face."*

— William Makepeace Thackeray

The Universe is alive with energy; nothing exists without it. Everything that you see—and most of what you don't—is full of waves and vibrations. No matter where you go or what you do, you're constantly sending and receiving energy, and you live in a confluence of unseen frequencies all the time. In fact, you're actually being pelted from all directions with television, radio, telephone, and satellite signals of every kind. All you need is the right apparatus set at the proper frequency in order to interpret them.

You resemble one of those satellites, picking up signals from other individuals and projecting ones of your own. You broadcast the energy that determines your consequences. You're wired for this, and whether you realize it or not, the results you've been getting are due to the vibrations of your own personal energy field. The beautiful thing about this is that if you don't like what's coming in, you're always free to change what you're sending out.

Energy is one of your primary powers, and it's behind several of the Universal Laws. It combines with consciousness to form the greatest generator of your destiny. By consciously choosing what kind of energy you want to project, you also determine what kind of consequences you receive. It's really a very simple process, and it's going on all the time.

In the physical world, the matching of frequencies is a phenomenon known as entrainment. When similar signals come together, they tend to vibrate as the same resonance; this is what creates the sense of attraction. It's not chemistry—it's matching energy. The principles apply across the board. Whether it's social, romantic, professional, or personal, you're destined to pull in what you put out. So in order to change what you attract, you need to figure out exactly how you create your personal energy field.

Our Big, Fat Energy Producers

Your electromagnetic vibrations are the resonance of your light energy, the frequency of your mind, heart, and soul. As we saw earlier, the biggest part of this can be found in your mind and feelings. But where do your thoughts and emotions come from? Do they just appear out of nowhere? What makes this part of your personal energy engine run?

The foundation of your emotional and cognitive power is formulated in your core conclusions. In fact, all that you manifest can be traced back to them. Simply put, your belief system is a network of fundamental assumptions that you've chosen to embrace as a result of your upbringing and personal experience.

Similar to the way they deal with their thoughts, most people don't examine what they hold to be true. We live with our belief system the same way we live with our language: We've been given it from birth, so it's all that we know. It's quite literally the framework for all that we experience, and we're so accustomed to it that it doesn't even occur to us to try something different. But when we live without a conscious awareness of our beliefs and how they affect our lives, we willingly give up our power to change.

❀ No matter what we've been taught or how we've been treated, our beliefs are a choice. As thinking adults, we always have the option to change them. We can choose for ourselves what represents our own truth—consciously releasing whatever perpetuates fear and negativity in our own vibration and in the world's. In terms of energy and consciousness creation, a healthier, happier belief is the bottom line of greater success in every arena.

Although the positive or negative nature of our vibrational energy is most powerfully expressed in our thoughts and emotions, underneath those are our fundamental beliefs. Obviously, judgmental, fatalistic, or otherwise negative convictions can create only negative emotions and thoughts. Positive ones—those that nurture the self and provide hope for the future—produce correspondingly uplifting feelings and ideas. This is, of course, the most desirable frequency to project, because this is what gets the wonderful results we're looking for.

Let's take a look at how these energy producers are connected. Our beliefs are the underlying conclusions from which all assumptions and free-floating thoughts derive. We develop these beliefs either directly (through what we've been taught) or indirectly (through how we've been treated by our parents and other authority figures). It doesn't matter that these teachings may be untrue, unhealthy, or even downright destructive; the source of their influence makes them absolutely true for us. Each belief creates related thoughts that elicit emotional reactions, all combining to create the predominant energy that you unknowingly broadcast throughout your life.

For example, you may have been given the tenet that money proves your worth. This is a core belief, resulting in a lot of corresponding thoughts and conclusions, such as *I'll never be able to approve of myself until I make lots more money,* and *I'm just a failure now.* Such toxic thoughts create devastating emotions, such as fear, desperation, and self-loathing. What are the energetic and real consequences of this process? Take a look at the example in the following chart.

Core Belief: It's really hard to make it in this world.		
Thought	**Emotions**	**Energy**
I don't have what it takes.	Shame, fear	Repulsive, resistant
There's never enough to go around.	Hopelessness, despair	Heavy, dark
Why does everyone else get the breaks?	Anger, envy	Abrasive, agitated

This is just one guiding belief, but when you look at this process, it becomes clear how powerful your fundamental assumptions about life can be. Through them, you create the emotional energy that sets the tone of your world. You set yourself up for success or failure, happiness or grief—and the cycle of energy and events won't change until *you* determine to embrace only the beliefs that honor and nurture you.

Place Your BETs

Some people resist creating new, positive beliefs. They think that doing so would be deluding themselves, denying a difficult reality in order to create a fantasy view of life. An even more skewed reason for not changing beliefs is the pretense of motivation. Many people assume that they're driven by their urgent and desperate convictions, and if they give up these negative precepts, they'll no longer be motivated to do what it takes to become a winner—but exactly the opposite is true.

When you change your belief system, you also change your resulting emotions and thoughts. This is the triple connection of energy production. A more positive belief system stimulates far greater enthusiasm and much more staying power.

But when your BETs (**b**eliefs, **e**motions, and **t**houghts) are negative, you're actually wagering your life on conclusions of failure and difficulty. Where's that likely to lead? You might as well stake your energy on the positive belief, because at least then you have a chance to make it true. If you BET on the negative, you can never win. In fact, because your BETs about the future permeate your consciousness, this destructive mentality creates the expectation (and believe it or not, on some strange level, even the *hope*) that the unfavorable outcome will appear. This is why it's so important to find out how your beliefs are keeping you down.

JOURNAL FOR SUCCESS

In order to become the master of your beliefs, answer the following questions in your journal. Give yourself some time to think things through and make clear decisions about the optional, honoring beliefs that could replace the old, negative ones.

- What are some of the things you've been taught to believe about yourself and your value?

- How do these conclusions make you feel?

- What alternative views can you now choose that will honor your value and produce healthier, more attractive energy in the world?

- What are some of the things that you've been taught to assume about other people and your relationship to them?

- How do these conclusions make you feel?

- What healthier, more honoring conclusions can you now embrace about others and your relationship to them?

- What are some of the things that you can do to remind yourself to choose these new beliefs on a daily basis?

Don't skip this exercise. Think honestly about your responses and come up with some creative options, because this is vital to your energy production. It only makes sense to BET on the positive—it's the only way good things can come up. If you're going to stake your life on something, place your wager on honoring **beliefs**, happier **emotions**, and optimistic **thoughts**. When you do, the Universe will be glad to pay up—and you may even find yourself winning the jackpot!

Test Your AQ

Your personal energy field is made up of your mental and emotional patterns, your beliefs and attitudes, and even the way you move and speak. This is the magnetic force behind your success experience. You may think that getting ahead depends on things such as your looks, how much money you make, or even your IQ. But ultimately it's none of these things. It's your *AQ*—your **a**ttraction **q**uotient—that really indicates whether or not you have the energy it takes to achieve on both personal and professional levels.

To get an indication of your own leanings, take the following quiz. Your AQ indicates your positive energy production and the resonant patterns of your magnetic attraction. Retake this test periodically to see how your vibration is changing.

ATTRACTION-QUOTIENT QUIZ

Rate the following questions on a scale of 1 to 10, with 1 being never and 10 being all the time. Write your rating on the line on the left—and be honest!

On a scale of 1 to 10, do you . . .

_____ 1. . . . have confidence in the things you do?

_____ 2. . . . feel that you know your personal purpose and are working in that direction?

_____ 3. . . . accept your looks and appearance right now?

_____ 4. . . . feel happy in your present circumstances?

_____ 5. . . . feel optimistic about your future?

_____ 6. . . . make your own goals and happiness a priority?

_____ 7. . . . feel willing to take risks?

_____ 8. . . . try to think positively when faced with difficult situations?

_____ 9. . . . value and appreciate the good things you already have in your life?

_____ 10. . . . respect your body by eating right and getting regular exercise?

_____ % (Add your score here to get your AQ.)

Don't be discouraged if your number is lower than you'd like. The most common scores for the AQ quiz fall between 50 and 75 percent. Whether yours is lower or higher, you can use this test as an opportunity to become aware of the energy changes you need to make in order to alter your life results.

To create a specific focus for positive signals, change all of the AQ quiz questions that received less than a 7 rating into positive intentions and affirmations. Use these on a daily basis to create a different momentum in your energy production. For example, if you gave only 5 points to question five, affirm: *I am feeling more and more optimistic about my future. I have the power to make my future better in every way.*

Write these statements on index cards to carry with you and read them often. Don't look at this as busywork, because it actually opens you to new ideas and approaches that could turn your energy around. You are—and always will be—the generator of your own success. Choose to broadcast a brighter vibration, and you're bound to tune in to brilliant results.

AFFIRMATIONS FOR ATTRACTIVE ENERGY

- *I am choosing a new, healthy, nurturing belief system for myself right now. It is my right—and my future.*

- *Only I choose what is true for me. From now on, I release any belief that is toxic or dishonoring in any way.*

- *As I think more positively, I send out better energy and attract better and better results.*

- *My own healthy and attractive energy is up to me. I choose to create a peaceful mentality now.*

- *I accept myself, my value, and my appearance. I make my own self-acceptance a priority.*

⊕ ⊕ ⊕

Chapter 11

THE POWER
OF INTENTION

The Fourth Personal Power of Success

---

*"Keep your thoughts on what you intend to create.
Stay consistently matched up with the field of intention,
and then watch for the clues that what you're summoning
from the all-creative Source is arriving in your life."*

— Dr. Wayne W. Dyer

Your intentions are key catalysts for the Laws of Desire and Intent. Nothing you do is without purpose, whether you're aware of it or not. When you have clear and honoring aims in both your daily life and the pursuit of your goals, you tap in to the natural forces of the Law of Pure Desire—and once again, consciousness is key. You must become aware of (and take control of) your intentions.

Any action, decision, or behavior that you choose to engage in could have a number of different objectives behind it. Although the deed may not change, a different intention can transform its energy completely, and therefore modify the consequences that you draw back into your life.

As an example, let's look at a common workplace situation that may seem positive on the surface but really depends on intention. Let's say that you give your supervisor a compliment. If you're expressing how you genuinely feel and you want to share something affirmative, then both the intention and the act are positive. This creates a genuinely honoring resonance, and only beneficial results will come back to you.

Let's say, however, that you're trying to use that compliment to butter up your boss and ingratiate yourself, perhaps hoping to get a raise or a good evaluation. In this case, your intention is manipulative, and your energy resonates with a dense and deceitful vibration. Of course, you may still get the raise or the good review, but eventually you're bound to magnetize something deceptive and controlling from someone else.

If your motivation to be kind in any situation is an attempt to gain approval or prove your own worth, you're essentially trying to manipulate acceptance and self-esteem. Such a dishonoring purpose can only negate the energy you send out, broadcasting a very clear message that you don't believe that you deserve to be valued for yourself. Your compliment (or any other caring act) may *seem* to be kind, but if it's made out of desperation, it completely reverses the energy. Such is the power of your intentions—to completely change your vibration and therefore the consequences of your life.

Everything you do is driven by this force. Whether you're eating breakfast, driving to work, writing a check, or doing your job, you're engaging in these activities with meaning. Even the most tedious task has intention underneath it. Of course there's the obvious purpose, but there's also an underlying energy that you may not be aware of. You may think that your goal for driving to work is simply to get there, but what is your intention for the *experience* of it? What kind of energy do you intend to engage in during this activity? It may be just a morning commute, but the way you go through it is important. Your obvious purpose for writing a check is to pay for something, but what is the energetic rationale behind that? It's not just the surface reasons that you have to consider; it's also the *intention of the experience.*

When you're driving to work, you can decide to enjoy the ride, or you can spend your time worrying about what you have to get done that day. While writing a check, you can choose to appreciate what you're paying for, or you can worry about how little money you have in your checking account. While doing your job, you can be grateful for the work you have and intend to do your best, or you can drag yourself through the day, resenting having to be there at all.

In performing these activities, which of the options do you think will garner the best results? Your mental intentions are a powerful force because they direct your consciousness creation. Think of how many experiences you go through each day with an undercurrent of negativity. You may think that it's no big deal, but this kind of approach to life creates a vicious energetic cycle. Fearful and resentful intentions and striving and manipulative behaviors create worry and depression—negative energies that only increase your misery.

Intend to Be Happy!

It's time to experience the activities of your life with a positive intention, to see each part of your reality with gratitude and trust, instead of the constant worry that overwhelms so many people. When fear and anxiety become your dominant emotions, their energy pervades your motivations. That's what happens when you're always thinking things such as *What if I can't pay the bills? What if I don't make the sale? I hate my job! I'm such a failure!* Over time, these and other negative thoughts will actually become your expectations.

You've probably heard of "self-fulfilling prophecies." Well, believe it or not, this phrase is scientifically sound. The focus of your emotional energy can actually transform the fear of some future problem into a subconscious plan to make that problem a reality. You may think your goal is wealth, but if you live in terror of poverty, that fear actually becomes your driving intention! The more you fear being poor, the more your negative vibration pushes away abundance. This is the energy dynamic of Paradoxical Intent; you must shift from desperation to determination.

You must work on your goals but intend to trust; plan to live happy now. Whether you're weeding in the garden or doing the laundry, get out of your negativity and aim to see the potential for joy in each and every task.

This is especially true in the pursuit of your dreams. Your intention for wealth—or any other good thing—must be pure, never driven by fear. People often ask me how to maintain a strong focus on their desires without falling into this emotional pit. Think of the energy difference between desperation and determination. The former is a fear-based need for your desired results. The latter, on the other hand, is the intention to take peaceful but persistent action in the direction of your dreams, all the while aiming to create happiness even now, without them.

These experiences are poles apart. You can feel a different vibration even when you just say the words *desperation* and *determination.* Shift your intention out of anguish and move to a more determined intention by surrendering your fearful attachments to the goal. When you become desperate, you've given way too much power to the result. But you can take back control by returning to a pure intention.

To figure out what kind of approach you're taking, look at these statements to see which group represents your energy the most:

DESPERATE INTENTIONS

- My goal (job, money, relationship, etc.) is what really will make me happy.

- I know that this achievement will make me a success.

- Reaching my desire will make me feel accepted.

- Only when I get ahead will I feel safe or secure.

- I have to hurry to make this happen. I can't stop working on this until everything's okay.

DETERMINED INTENTIONS

- I have the power to make myself happy.

- I can reach my goals later and still feel successful today.

- I can choose to accept myself now.

- I have the power to feel safe and secure in the present moment.

- I have the power to create all these positive emotions and experiences even now. I can choose trust right away and let go of the fear.

As you read the statements, you can feel the different energy that each set produces. Surrendering the fearful, emotional attachments to your goals will be a crucial part of shifting to a more peaceful, receptive vibration. A positive consciousness and a trusting, optimistic purpose will create the magnetic resonance that draws your desires to you. You must surrender your need for your goal in order to magnetize it more quickly. This is achieved when you embrace your emotional intentions for happiness, success, and acceptance in the present moment.

Never obsess about any one way to achieve your emotional dreams; open yourself up to all the options that may be available to create those feelings right now. When you get anxious about a specific goal, visualize the outcome you desire with enthusiasm and optimism. Then affirm: *I am drawing this or something better to my life right now.* This will awaken you to the abundant options in all of your pursuits. Surrender and trust in the open outcome of your desires. There's no more magnetic energy than trust and flexibility—and no greater way to turn your intentions into reality.

JOURNAL FOR SUCCESS

In order to genuinely surrender, you must look inside for your real intentions. Ask yourself these questions both in meditation and in your journal:

- When I think of my desires, what are my emotions? Do I feel worry and fear or optimism and hope?

- What emotional (*not* financial) outcome do I intend this goal to bring to my life? What can I do or think to create this state of being right now?

- Is my purpose fear based or manipulative in any way? Does it increase or decrease my own sense of dignity and honor?

- Is my intention optimistic—not only for future outcomes but also for present activities? If not, why not? What other option can I choose?

- Are the intentions around my goal conflicting in any way? If so, what positive and pure motivation can I focus my energy on now?

Open, Clear, and Unconflicted

Since your intentions are your Universal order forms, you must be very specific, sure, and optimistic. Being unclear would be like going into a restaurant and just telling the waitress, "I'm hungry." You have to be aware of what you want and let the Universe know exactly what it is. Conflicting thoughts spell doom, even for long-held desires. You must live with certain knowledge and strong belief, telling yourself: *I can do this. I'm going to do this. I deserve it!* There's no room for questions or contradictions—only a pure, straightforward intention.

Whether it's about your abilities or worthiness, you can't muddy your Universal order with negativity and resistance. Consider what would happen if you went into a restaurant and told the waitress, "Well, I'd like the steak, but maybe I should just have a hamburger. . . but a steak sounds so good. . . ." She'd give up and walk away.

But let's say that she gives you a second chance. This time you say, "I'd really like the lobster, but I don't deserve to spend that much money on myself. I guess I'll just get a fish sandwich . . . but I'd really love the lobster!" Eventually the waitress won't even come back!

The Universe is the same way. If you're constantly shifting from one intention to another, from desire to disbelief, it just can't know what to serve—so it won't give you anything! You may think, *I want a new relationship,* but also think, *I've been hurt so many times.* You may hope that you get a big promotion, but you may also fear that the other candidates are more qualified. Such conflicting approaches poison your energy and cloud your consciousness, turning away the Universal flow. *Your intentions must be clear, unconflicted, and open to receiving.* Maintain a strong vision of your goal and send it out before you. The Universe is waiting to fill your order, but you have to let it know what you want.

Create an ongoing consciousness about your intentions—not just about your long-term goals, but also about your daily life. For example, when I consider the day ahead, my first intention is to create happiness and value in all that I do, and I work on sharing those energies with others. As I begin a new activity, I try to plan my emotional approach. Since every single thing you do has a focus that directs your energy production, you need to be fully aware of your real motivations, especially those about magnetizing greater success.

TIPS FOR POWERFUL INTENTION

You can have more control over your energy production by incorporating these pointers for powerful intentions each day:

- **Spend a few minutes each morning meditating on or writing about your intentions for that day.** See yourself going through your planned activities with a clear awareness of your purpose for each activity—and make it positive, optimistic, and joyful. By doing so, you're projecting a brighter consciousness out into the world and intending a happy, successful day.

- **Focus your intentions many times a day.** If you're experiencing a difficult time or working on a challenging project, renew your conscious direction as often as possible. Take a break midmorning, at lunch, or after work to create a positive intention for the next few hours.

- **Try to engage in more positive intentions during the mundane activities of your life.** Be aware of your mental direction as you're doing such things as eating, driving, and performing household chores. Find a positive, heartfelt purpose in the experience of every single task, and it will change the nature of your energy completely.

- **In the evening, consciously create an intention for your nighttime energy.** Affirm: *Tonight I will sleep soundly. I will wake up relaxed, refreshed, and enthusiastic, looking forward to the day.*

- **Reevaluate your goal intentions periodically.** Make sure you're not creating conflict around your desires by clouding them with fear. Stay focused, open, determined, and optimistic in order to keep your desires on track.

Your intentions lay the groundwork for your future success, so don't let them get tangled up in doubt and confusion. Never negate your abilities or dismiss your worthiness—and never, ever minimize the great abundance of Universal possibilities. A pure desire knows that your goal is available and achievable. You deserve it, so intend it!

AFFIRMATIONS FOR A PURE AND POWERFUL INTENTION

- *I am beginning to take a closer look at why I do the things I do. I understand that my intentions are powerful forces in my life.*

- *I have the power to make myself happy. This is my responsibility and my present intention.*

- *I am open to the abundant options the Universe has to offer. There are plenty of ways to make my dreams come true.*

- *Every day I am becoming more aware of all my intentions. I choose to live every day based in trust and love.*

- *I bring a joyful, conscious intention to all that I do—even the daily tasks of life.*

⊕ ⊕ ⊕

Chapter 12

THE POWER OF CHOICE

The Fifth Personal Power of Success

"You are free to choose, but the choices you make today will determine what you will have, be, and do in the tomorrow of your life."

— Zig Ziglar

The dynamic personal power that links all the others is *choice*. Unfortunately, we're often so stuck in our habits that we may be completely unaware that our options always remain open. This is true from our seemingly insignificant and mundane picks to our most monumental, life-altering decisions.

A lot of times we limit ourselves according to the circumstances of our lives. We think, *I can't leave my job because I have to pay the mortgage.* We assume that we can't move into a new occupation just because of an old decision to pursue the one we're in. We're often compelled to keep sticking with the same thing over and over simply because we've done so in the past.

We're also inclined to limit our choices according to the patterns we've been taught. We think that we don't have the option to stand up for ourselves because we were never given the chance in the past. We continue to *choose* to be people pleasers because that was the path we saw others take. We rely on the habits of our social conventions, past ways of doing things, and long-held manners of speaking, eating, learning, communicating, and prioritizing. Day after day, we make thousands of choices, but it rarely occurs to us that we have the ability to do everything differently—if we so desire.

I once heard a funny story about a woman who made delicious roasts and gravies. The meat was so tender that it would almost melt in your mouth. She'd learned how to cook them from her mother, and she passed the tradition down to her daughter, saying that one of the keys to a juicy roast was to cut the ends off before putting it in the roaster. Her daughter obediently did this and followed her directions to the letter, and she, too, was able to make a delicious dinner.

One day when she was visiting her grandmother—the woman who'd come up with the recipe to begin with—she said, "I'm so glad that mom told me your secret. Everybody thinks I make the juiciest roasts in town."

Her grandmother asked, "What secret is that?"

"Cutting the ends off the roast, of course!" the girl answered. "Mom's been doing it since she started cooking. She does it because you did it that way, and your roasts were always delicious, too."

Upon hearing that, the old grandmother laughed and laughed. When she finally composed herself, she told her granddaughter, "Honey, I didn't cut the ends off the roast because it made it juicier. I did it because my oven was so small that I couldn't fit the whole thing in at one time!"

This is a funny but very revealing illustration of why we often continue to make the same choices throughout our lives: They become habits that we maintain without consciousness. There may have been good reasons for them originally, but do we really get any benefit from continuing to pick the same things now? This is an important question, because so many of the decisions we've become locked into have the power to affect the energy—and even the very quality—of our lives.

✳ In every single moment we face an energetic choice of some kind. Not only do we decide what to do, we also determine what to think, believe, feel, and perceive about the situations we're in. In the long run, it's our daily choices that come together to create the tapestry of our existence. Our moment-to-moment decisions weave the picture of who we are and what we become. These are really our defining moments, the ongoing little decisions that determine the energy and direction of our lives.

Where our patterns are concerned, we have to understand that we don't just make a decision once, we do so over and over again. You may have decided to smoke when you were a teenager, but every time you light up, you're actually making that monumental agreement all over again. Every single time it's a new choice, even when you're not at all conscious of it. Unfortunately, your lack of awareness doesn't diminish its power in your life.

Our days are filled with countless unconscious choices and hundreds of conscious ones, and our unconsidered actions have just as much power as the decisions we spend a long time thinking about. In fact, these choices can be so habitual that they're likely to have an even greater impact! But when we take control of all our possibilities, we begin to direct the energetic momentum of our lives. This power, this ability to choose, allows us to orchestrate the success of our desires in two fundamental ways—in our choice of attitude and action.

Attitude and Action

The choices you make always revolve around one of two things, attitude or action. The former is inherently linked to your perception and beliefs, the two fundamental pieces of consciousness and energy. In this way, your attitude is a primary catalyst both to what you magnetize and what you manifest; it's the subtle combination of thought and emotion focused on a particular issue.

We may say that we have a good attitude (or a bad one), but we have to look more closely at what this really means. In most cases, the good is based on positive convictions and uplifting emotions; the bad arises from pessimistic conclusions combined with fearful or hostile feelings.

You may have had some horrible attitudes in the past, but you don't have to embrace them any longer. Your mentality creates your reality, and where the laws of success are concerned, attitude *is* everything. This is energetically true because your outlook is the propellant of your consciousness creation. It may not have occurred to you before, but you choose how you approach every day—in fact, every moment. So choose a new positive attitude right now.

It's also a good idea to investigate the decisions you make concerning your actions. There are three main courses of action you pursue all the time, and those are your consistent behaviors concerning yourself, others, and your goals. These have the power to enhance your life or destroy it, so if you're not pursuing behavioral options that are honoring and healthy, it's time to start making new choices now.

JOURNAL FOR SUCCESS

Think about the attitudes and actions that you engage in concerning the following issues. Write your answers in your journal, and then determine to apply more positive choices to your daily life.

Attitude Choices:

1. What's your attitude about your present work situation?

    *   What are your thoughts about it? Do they tend to be positive or negative?

    *   How do you *feel* about your job? Do you generally feel good or bad about it?

    *   What can you change about your thoughts or beliefs that can make your feelings and attitude about work more positive?

2. What's your attitude about money?

- What are the thoughts and emotions you have concerning money?

- Do these make you feel satisfied and happy or urgent and needy?

- How can you redefine your beliefs about money to create better feelings about it?

3. What's your attitude about pursuing your goals?

- List a few of your most dominant thoughts related to each goal.

- How do you feel about your goals? Do you tend to be hopeful and resolute or doubtful and hesitant?

- Write down positive intentions and conclusions to reverse any negative feelings you may have about these topics.

Create the intention to *only* engage in beliefs and emotions that will broadcast a healthier consciousness and more attractive energy concerning all these issues. Remind yourself of these options every day; read your new conclusions and affirm your new positive attitudes often.

Action Choices:

1. Self-action:

- What behaviors do you engage in on a daily basis that might be considered dishonoring to you? (Include eating, drinking, how you talk to yourself, and how you spend your time.)

- List some new choices that would create a more positive lifestyle and higher energy to attract better results.

- What can you do to implement some of these new choices on a regular basis? Write down some suggestions and refer to them often.

- What are the behaviors and actions that you engage in on a regular basis that tend to honor you and your way of living?

- What can you do to make these choices more often?

2. Actions toward others:

- Which of the following adjectives best describe the kind of actions you engage in toward others most frequently? Circle one from each pair.

Loving	Unloving
Trusting	Fearful
Accepting	Judgmental
Flexible	Controlling
Tolerant	Abrasive
Peaceful	Hostile

- Why do you think that you choose these types of actions?

- What kind of energy do they create?

- If you circled any item from the right-hand column, what different choices could you make in both your beliefs and behaviors that would create a more harmonic resonance?

3. Goal actions:

- How often do you take action toward your goals?

- When making the choice between acting on your dreams or on something else, what usually takes precedence?

- How *enthusiastic* are you when you engage in goal-oriented actions?

- What can you do to take more frequent and more energetic action toward these desires?

To succeed at your goals, you must often choose them over other things, and this is where the power of choice connects with the power of letting go. You may have to release some habit or even personal gratification in order to make your goal your highest choice. In fact, no matter what the issue is, if you're really conscious about your life, you'll find that time and time again you have the option to positively apply both of these principles. This is one of the most liberating and empowering decisions you can make: *the choice to let go.*

How many times a day are you given the chance to either hold on or relax your grip? Whether it's a spontaneous habit, a negative thought pattern, or a difficult emotion such as fear or anger, you always have the option to either clutch it to you or cast it aside. Yet so many people feel compelled to hang on because they think that doing so is what gives them their power. They hold on to their habits, other people, their titles, their comfort zones, and even their possessions. But setting these things free actually gives you your ultimate power.

When you choose to let go, you free yourself of attachment, fear, and the need for control—and with each of these decisions you gain *more* strength. Especially determine to let go of your old negative patterns, attitudes, and habits. If they haven't gotten you where you want to be so far, they obviously aren't working, so you must choose some new ones now.

Choice or Consequence

In the rhythm of your life, every moment is a choice—and every one of them has a consequence. In fact, each choice has two kinds: actual and energetic. Sometimes the actual results are easy to see. For example, if you keep overeating, you'll gain weight. That's the actual, physical result. But what's the energetic outcome? The resonance of the decision to overindulge is dishonoring, sending messages of self-dismissal and self-loathing, a resonance that's bound to attract people and situations who'll promote even more of those feelings.

There are many times, however, where the conclusions aren't so clear. Whether you're making a phone call, ordering a meal, or hiring a vice president, it's important to consider both the actual and energetic consequences of your choice. You may not always be able to predict the outcome, but you need to weigh the options and look at the energy involved before you decide. Your choices must ring true for you, and to achieve that end, they must resonate with dignity, integrity, and self-honoring.

When you're choosing a course of action—big or small—there are two questions that will help reveal the energetic nature of the consequences. Ask yourself: *Does this choice honor me? Does it enhance my sense of dignity and maintain my integrity?* If you can answer yes to these questions, then whatever that decision may be, you'll know that you're going with the highest option possible. The Universe longs to support your honoring energy, so you can rest assured that every choice you make with this intention will bring genuine power and ever-increasing blessings!

⊕

AFFIRMATIONS FOR HEALTHY, HAPPY, AND POWERFUL CHOICES

- *I know that I have countless choices every day. I bring my consciousness to each of them.*

- *All of my daily decisions define me and determine my energy. I make loving and honoring choices in thought, word, and deed each day.*

- *I choose more positive attitudes toward myself, my goals, and my life.*

- *I always choose to engage in a more empowering and loving perception of myself.*

- *I choose to live free of fear, worry, envy, or judgment. I choose to let go and live in peace.*

⟐ ⟐ ⟐

Chapter 13

THE POWER OF LOVE

The Sixth Personal Power of Success

"Love is an essential ingredient for success. Without it, your life suffers in emptiness. With it your life vibrates with warmth and satisfaction."

— Glenn Van Ekeren

When I talk about the power of love to my business clients, they often balk. One man in management said, "You had me right up to this point. The science of it all makes perfect sense, but when you talk about love, you lose me."

This is a common reaction. When people understand the human application of quantum physics, they can see that their consciousness, energy, and intention carry great power in the consequences of their lives. But when it comes to success, most people want to know, "What's love got to do with it?"

Love is a very real power within both the Universe and individuals. It's an energy that can be deeply felt, not just romantically, but in every way; its strong, vibrating, creative force moves freely and fluidly throughout the world. When we align our own personal energy of love with this Universal current, there's nothing that we can't achieve.

This vibration is the absence of hate and fear. The choice to experience, perceive, and promote love causes you to see the real value in your life and draws more worth back to you. The energy not only accelerates the achievement of your goals, it creates a profoundly happy resonance that permeates your entire life. Every time you choose to approach anything with love, you stimulate the action of all the Laws of Success, so let's look at how you can use this power to harness the force of each one.

1. The Law of Manifestation. To establish a loving consciousness, step back and choose a persistently peaceful and caring perception of yourself and others. This stimulates the creation of a personal reality filled with joy! In addition, when you're more aware of all the forms of love in your life, your observation of it increases kind responses from the Universe, manifesting abundantly wonderful experiences.

2. The Law of Magnetism. Love is the single most magnetic energy that you can project. Unfortunately, fear and hate can also be pretty attractive—in all the wrong ways. In the pursuit of success, these negative energies can never pull in anything pleasant or valuable. When you choose a loving attitude, you release the confusion, worry, and doubt. So take a deep breath, let go of all your concerns, and affirm: *I choose love.* Your personal energy will have a brilliantly attractive vibration.

3. The Law of Pure Desire. A loving heart is full of hope and excitement. Genuine affection for yourself ensures your belief in your future and your goal. And when you choose to embrace your life right now, you're much more able to surrender your attachment to your goals. This purifies your desire and greatly accelerates your results.

4. The Law of Paradoxical Intent. Loving intentions are free from fear. Instead of worry, trust becomes your way of life—and your predominant energy. You can bring caring intentions to all that you do, whether you're working, playing, eating, talking, thinking, or even just breathing. To do so, all you have to do is say the word *love* itself.

5. The Law of Harmony. The key to harmony—and the magic of synchronicity—is to live with honoring and loving acceptance. Choose to release judgment and hostility, both toward yourself and others. Open yourself to tolerance, forgiveness, and compassion, too. All of these will harmonize you with the mystical forces of synchronicity and reveal a Universe of opportunities.

6. The Law of Right Action. Bringing loving treatment to the world is the ultimate right action. The world responds and brings this back to you in the form of assistance, support, and blessings. When you're in a situation where you don't know what to do, ask yourself, *How do I bring love to this experience?* Then do it.

7. The Law of Expanding Influence. Your intention to spread loving energy expands your positive and peaceful life experience—and that of everyone around you. In your family, business dealings, social life, and community, your choice to engage in caring thoughts and actions expands the peace in the world. It also brings greater serenity and prosperity back to you, so you can then send more out and keep the eternal cycle going.

Let the Love Flow

No matter what Universal Law you're working with, you simply can't go wrong when you make the choice to spread love throughout your life. As always, the best place to start is with the self. Without the power of self-love, you can only live in fear and trepidation, and nothing positive can be promoted in that state of mind.

    ❋   This is a central energetic point: Self-love is not arrogant or conceited; it's the starting point of your ability to value everything and everyone around you. To stimulate this personal source of power, look in the mirror and affirm that you love, value, and appreciate yourself. Stop looking for the faults, and start acknowledging your good qualities.

> Love is a strong, pulsating vibration. If you refuse to cherish yourself, you send out an abrasive energy that causes others to refuse to care for you, also. Make no mistake about this——you simply can't engage in self-loathing and succeed.

In addition to affirming yourself, it's also a good idea to do nice things for yourself. Create an atmosphere at home and work that inspires you. Periodically throughout your day, take a few minutes to relax and regroup; give yourself the encouragement to keep going and say congratulations for a job well done. To attract caring responses from the Universe, you must choose love in all its meanings and apply it to all things. Treasure the day, the sights around you, and the tasks and activities you're engaged in. Your self-encouragement and life appreciation will attract the same wonderful vibrations from other people and from the world.

Once you've established your own self-loving energy, you can extend it by channeling it into the hearts of those around you. Smile sincerely and send affection through your gaze as you make eye contact with a friend; feel it moving out your fingers as you shake someone's hand. Intend it in your voice and your movements in every activity, great or small. Visualize a bright, passionate energy flowing like a rainbow from your heart to those of others.

Sometimes, if you're just feeling too tired or if you encounter people who stimulate some lower emotions, you may find it difficult to visualize sending your own caring energy to them. In this case, you can choose to be a channel of the Universal vibration that's always present. See yourself as a funnel with great waves of Divine love pouring into you and then flowing out from your own heart center. When you do so, you make yourself the pipeline from one source of love to another, and this puts you right in the center of the magical current of loving, beneficial intention.

BROADCASTING-LOVE PROCESS

If you're having difficulties with a situation or another person, sending loving energy in that direction is a very valuable tool for resolution. Begin by thinking of what you're dealing with, and then relax and gently send loving energy there. Move out all negativity such as anger and fear; just release it and let it go—then replace it with the word *love.*

Take a few deep breaths and just repeat "love" over and over again. You may resist this if you're dealing with an abrasive person or a difficult problem, but let that opposition go. Breathe deeply and surrender the relationship or situation to the caring Universe.

Keep breathing deeply and gently, repeating the word *love,* then say a prayer for the highest and best resolution for all. In time, you'll start to feel your own emotions changing, and if you repeat this process whenever the issue comes to mind, you'll see a shift in the situation, too.

I've done this process on many occasions with amazing results. Several years ago, for instance, I rented some elaborate recording equipment for a seminar I was doing out of town. I was going to need it for two weeks, so the fee was rather expensive. A few days after I'd picked it up, when I was getting ready to leave for my trip, I decided to test the equipment to make sure that it worked.

Unfortunately, it didn't. Every time I recorded, it left a loud buzzing noise on the tape, so I called the rental studio. I told them what happened and that I'd be returning the equipment that day. Mike, the man who ran the place, told me that I could bring it in, but I would *not* be getting my money back. He said that I needed to make the return within 24 hours of picking it up in order to get a refund.

I explained that it had only been two days instead of one, and asked if I could at least get some of my money, but he was adamant: 24 hours was the rule, and they wouldn't change the policy for any reason. We got into a bit of a heated discussion, and I told him that I'd be returning everything that day anyway. His final statement to me was, once again: "You can bring it in, but you're not going to get your money back."

When I got in the car to drive over, I was fuming because I felt that Mike was being unfair and inflexible. After all, it was his equipment that was faulty. But when I started driving, I reconsidered. I said to myself, *I'm going to send some love to this situation and see what happens.*

The studio was about a half hour away from my home, and I spent the entire time sending loving thoughts to that manager. I visualized myself dispatching comments of care and appreciation in the direction of the studio, and I repeated the word *love* over and over again.

I continued to do this as I did some deep breathing, and slowly but surely I felt myself calming down. By the time I was halfway there, I genuinely felt peaceful, willing to accept whatever happened. I wasn't going to let any amount of money ruin my peace of mind or my tranquil heart. I continued with the process, repeating the word *love* along with Mike's name and the name of the studio, although I didn't really care anymore. My motivation was no longer to see if I could get my money back, only to bring harmony to a situation where two people were at odds.

When I arrived, I carried the equipment in and asked to see Mike. I remember feeling a sense of resignation because he'd been so firm in his final comment to me. When he came out, he started to investigate the machinery, asking me what had been wrong. I didn't confront, attack, or try to manipulate him in any way. I just explained the problem and continued to send love.

Then he looked at me and said, "I've never done this before, but I'm going to give you a break." I thought I was going to get a little bit of my rental fee back, and I was very appreciative. But it was even better than that: Mike gave me a full refund of *all* my money. Not only that, he gave me a free recording tape! When he took the equipment into the back, the man working at the counter who'd overheard our discussion told me, "He's never done that before. I don't know what you said to make him change his mind."

What I'd said was the word *love*—over and over again, in my mind and out loud, right in his direction. That was only one of the countless times I've seen this process work. I've used it in professional and personal situations and in my counseling, too. In one case, I was doing marriage counseling with two people who were driving each other (and me) crazy. He was a penny-pincher, and she was a spendthrift. I told them that they were each making the issue of money mean too much, but it seemed that nothing I said could get them to stop arguing about it, so I finally decided to try sending them love. In the morning before our sessions, on the drive to work, and whenever I thought about them, I would say and broadcast love.

It took a few weeks, but one day they came in with an entirely different attitude. They said I'd been right when I told them that they needed to meet in the middle and make their relationship the priority instead of the money. After months of head butting, they picked up on the energy of love that I was sending them, and they finally decided to give it to each other.

> ※ Love brings peace to animosity and resolution to difficulty. It's one of the most powerful intentions you can make and one of the most beneficial actions you take. Say it, feel it, and allow it to be your own gentle attitude. Make love a real presence in your conscious life, and you'll soon be more conscious of a wonderfully loving reality.

Try this for yourself. The next time something comes up that you can't find an answer for, send love to it. When a problem arises with someone in your life, send love to them. Or even when nothing in particular is going on, just stop, close your eyes, and breathe in the word and its energy. This isn't just some fluffy, feel-good farce; it's *real* energetic power. Love changes your consciousness and frequency—and even your physiology. It activates your heart center like nothing else, fueling your emotional powerhouse. When you bring your heart and your head together in loving purpose, the river of abundance will flow right to your door.

AFFIRMATIONS FOR LIVING IN LOVE

- *I live with a consciousness of love. I see myself and my life with loving eyes.*

- *In my attitude toward myself and others, I choose love.*

- *I release judgment, criticism, and conflict. I choose peace.*

- *I send my love to all that I see. Many times a day, I think, feel, and say the word "love" with a heartfelt intention.*

- *I happily look for the opportunity to help others, show compassion, and be of service in little and big ways.*

⊕ ⊕ ⊕

PART III

THE FIVE MAGNETIC ENERGIES OF SUCCESS

Success isn't just a random occurrence that happens to a lucky few; it's a consciousness creation that comes from your personal alignment with the Universal Laws. What seems like chance is really energetic synchronicity, a process of entraining—or matching—your own vibration with that of the Universal flow. A constant stream of blessings is always available from that mighty river, and there's only one thing that can stop it from flowing in your direction—your own personal resonance.

But take heart! Whatever you've resonated up till now, whatever you've attracted, there are still some significant energies that you can engage in that will help you connect your own personal energy field with that wonderfully abundant infinite realm of all possibilities. When you choose to bring these magnetic forces into your heart and mind on a daily basis, you'll create a major shift in consciousness and an entirely different resonance. Your images and vibrations will change. Your view of yourself and your life will take on a higher, grander understanding, and you'll open yourself to receiving truly awe-inspiring results.

Chapter 14

THE ENERGY OF CONFIDENCE

The First Magnetic Energy of Success

"We can change our whole life and the attitude of people around us simply by changing ourselves."

— Rudolf Dreikurs

When you're talking about success, the first and foremost magnetic energy is that of self-confidence. In fact, lack of it is one of the biggest reasons people don't succeed—not because they can't, but because they don't believe in their own worth and abilities. How do you see yourself? Do you believe that you're worthy and able? This is what confident energy is all about!

But if you're the kind of person who's never really felt that way, you can still change things. No matter what you've felt like, or even how you've performed in the past, you do have the power to create the confidence you need now. There's no energy pattern that you can't change, and if you're willing to give it a little time and effort, you can use all the powers discussed in Part II to completely transform your view of yourself!

Sometimes confidence can be selective. For example, we may feel good about participating in a sport but lack security in the business world; we may be sure of ourselves at work yet feel totally incapable when it comes to romance. Generally speaking, though, we tend to know whether or not we have the kind of confidence it takes to really be a success.

What do you feel about yourself regarding this issue? Are you sure about your capability to succeed, or do you struggle with hesitation and self-doubt? Confidence seems to be an elusive commodity that few people understand and even fewer know how to consciously create. But when you look at the quantum mechanics of it, you'll realize that it's not only doable, it's necessary.

⚛ The source of your confidence comes largely from your self-image—and image is a key ingredient in consciousness creation. How you see yourself is intrinsically connected to what you expect of yourself. If you have a negative picture, you'll assume that you're going to perform poorly, and it's likely your reality will meet those assumptions. But if you have a positive, healthy self-image, you'll expect the best of yourself, and your consciousness will create that reality. In terms of consciousness creation, your self-perception moves outward to create your personal results.

Here's an example of how this works. Let's say that you had difficulty speaking in public when you were younger. In a high school speech class, you suffered through a few disastrous experiences where you had anxiety and stuttered all through your presentation. That caused you to perceive yourself as a failure in this area, and now you expect that "truth" to continue throughout your life.

Many years later, if someone were to ask you to give a speech at work, you'd have a spontaneous image of your past defeats, and even though you weren't actually in the process of stuttering in front of a group at that time, you'd immediately produce the neuropeptides that matched the unpleasant, fearful emotions from the past. This would further cement your poor self-image concerning this issue.

Sounds like an impossible cycle, doesn't it? Failure leads to negative image . . . which leads to more failure. But don't despair; there's good news. Once again, the quantum mechanics of energy and physiology gives us the power to change things from the inside out. No matter what's happened in the past, you always have the option to access a new neural network, create a brand-new image, and redefine any personal issue.

How can this be? Remember that the brain can't distinguish between an image of experience and one of vivid imagination. The visual cortex relies only partially on what is being seen. The bulk of our visual experience is made up of both the memories of past images and personal information forming specific expectations. If you change the scenes in your expectations, you can change your observable reality, as well as your consciousness creation!

I utilized this imagery and awareness shift while working with a client who was dealing with his own phobia of public speaking. Tom had come to see me at the age of 35, when he was faced with a dilemma at work. He'd moved up the corporate ladder rather rapidly and was now up for a promotion on a national level. There was only one problem: He was going to have to give presentations to large auditoriums filled with people, the mere thought of which paralyzed him with panic.

He'd always had a fear of public speaking, but had reached a tolerable level of comfort in conducting small meetings in groups of five or ten people held in conference rooms. Even that had been difficult at first, but he took medication and somehow managed to get through it. Now he'd have to speak to groups of hundreds—eventually even a few thousand—and just the idea of it threw him into horrendous panic attacks that the medication couldn't even touch.

When he came to see me, he told me about his past experiences with an attitude of hopeless resignation. He thought I was crazy when I told him, "Tom, we're going to change your history." When he asked me how, I answered, "Simple—by changing your imagery."

I began by teaching him some relaxation techniques, along with affirmations releasing his attachment to his past conclusions and images, which he used whenever the old thoughts came to mind. Then we started the process of creating some new visuals—as well as some fresh emotions to go along with them.

We did this through a series of hypnosis sessions, starting with a relaxing induction, followed by the visualization of a new, successful image.

We used a process called mental desensitization, where the picture would change somewhat with each consecutive session, expanding on the previous one and adding new elements of success and emotion each time.

In the first session, we created a scene where Tom was standing on a stage in a large auditorium. He was totally alone; there was no one in the audience or with him onstage. Since the room was empty, he saw himself speaking with complete confidence, comfort, and even enjoyment.

In the next session, he pictured only one person in the audience. I told him to choose someone who was supportive and encouraging, and he picked his wife. Again, he saw himself speaking with ease and enthusiasm. In his mind, his wife smiled up at him, laughed at all his jokes, and applauded at the end of his imaginary speech.

We repeated these two safe scenarios before we moved on, but then we slowly added more people to the picture: first, his children; next, his friends and other family members; and then some supportive co-workers from his office. With each and every "take," he saw himself as a powerful speaker, relaxed and engaging; and each time, we attached feelings of enjoyment, comfort, and relaxation. It took several sessions, but eventually Tom imagined himself speaking to an entire audience filled with people—and he saw himself having fun while he was doing it!

He did these imagery exercises in my office, and we made tape recordings for him to listen to every night at home. After about six months, it was time for the real thing. Tom was scheduled to address a group of around 700 people—at least 70 times larger than any other meeting he'd ever conducted. He was nervous, but excited, too. He continued smiling, relaxing, breathing deeply, and reliving the revised images, complete with the new emotions of enjoyment, comfort, and success. He never realized it, but he was now accessing a fresh neural network, producing different neuropeptides and entirely altered feelings.

His presentation was a great success; he was relaxed and funny, and he didn't even need the medication he'd been using in the little conference-room meetings. Tom got the promotion, along with a big raise and stock options to go with it—and since then, he's moved up even further! Now he conducts seminars in front of thousands without even thinking twice. His modified images created a new consciousness, biochemistry, and reality.

Whatever problems you may be facing, and whatever negative self-images may be haunting you, they *can* be turned around. The images that you now embrace about yourself only represent a certain part of your history, not your truth—or your future. They may seem accurate because they're familiar, and they may even feel irresistible because of their strong emotional content. But don't be deterred by these false assumptions.

Use your power of letting go to release the old limitations, and then employ your powers of choice and consciousness to create new, strong self-images. The following investigation will help you identify and release your negative self-images. Continue the process until you've created fresh pictures that will be the source of your new, exciting, and successful reality.

SHIFTING SELF-IMAGE

Begin by listing some of the images that you now have of yourself, then identify each one as either negative or positive according to the way it makes you feel. (For example: A good golfer—positive; overweight—negative; a kind person—positive; an alcoholic—negative.) Add and identify more images as you think of them, and follow these steps for each one:

- **For every negative image that you listed, write down the corresponding pessimistic conclusion or belief.** (For example: I'm too fat, and I'll never be able to lose weight. People don't like overweight people, so I'll never really succeed.)

- **Write some releasing affirmations related to each particular conclusion.** (For example: I release any image or judgment about my weight. I deserve to be accepted as I am. My new picture of myself is healthy, strong, and attractive.)

- **Write down a vivid description of each new positive image, filling it with colorful and happy details.** (For example: I see myself dressed beautifully and looking better than ever. I'm wearing an attractive outfit, and I notice that I'm looking more fit. I always see myself smiling, happy, and confident.)

- **Visualize your new images.** First do some deep breathing to relax, then picture all of the details of your new scene with joy. See the entire thing as brightly and clearly as possible. Hold the image very close and make it colorful; continue to relax and breathe deeply as you bring it even closer to you. Smile and attach uplifting emotional words to this view, such as *fun, beautiful, strong,* and *enjoyable.*

- **Let yourself reexperience this positive image for at least five or ten minutes each day.** Hold it close and feel it becoming more and more familiar to you. Know that this represents your *true* reality. The new pictures and loving emotions will bring confidence, greater happiness, and more successful results in every area of your life.

Only *you* can decide how to perceive, define, and imagine yourself. Your old negative conclusions were formed out of past experiences, but you can create new ones now. This is a different time, a fresh opportunity to reinvent yourself from the inside out. Since the Law of Magnetism shows that the world can only regard you in the exact same way that you see yourself, it's time to let go of the old self-judgments and make the choice to regard yourself highly *now.*

Support that with a positive change in perception and self-image, and your shift in consciousness will be complete. You'll create a sparkling new reality when you consciously determine to see yourself as valuable, capable, and deserving. In every single moment, you have the option to paint another picture of yourself, to embrace a new image, and to broadcast a vibrant and magnetic personal energy—so choose confidence now and always. Honor yourself in every thought, and you can confidently move toward a magnificent future.

AFFIRMATIONS FOR CHARISMATIC CONFIDENCE

- *I am choosing to think more highly of myself. I know that I deserve my own high regard.*

- *I affirm myself with a gentle and loving voice each day.*

- *I believe in myself. I value my integrity and my worth.*

- *I love my life and my self-loving energy. I am valuable and special just as I am.*

- *I choose to believe only the best about myself. I am learning to love and accept myself without conditions. I have all that I need to create what I want.*

⊕   ⊕   ⊕

Chapter 15

THE ENERGY OF OPTIMISM

The Second Magnetic Energy of Success

---

*". . . see it [the thing you want] as an existent fact—
and anything you can rightly wish for is yours."*

— Robert Collier

The second important magnetic energy is optimism, the attitude of positive assumption and the overall expectation that everything's going to be okay. It's closely connected to the subject of the previous chapter, confidence, because it's simpler for an optimistic person to be self-confident, and it's much easier for a confident person to be optimistic. So your decision to work on either of these energies is bound to enhance the other one as well.

There's a special kind of charge to optimism, a peaceful assurance that no matter what may be going on now, the world's going to send good things your way. This hopeful expectation is an important part of your consciousness PIE, because positive expectations project a dynamic and creative awareness. An optimistic outlook turns hope into reality and produces a vibrant and beautiful energy that draws Universal blessings.

Plodding in Fear Versus Prospering in Flow

Pessimists fill their consciousness with worry—although they may not even be aware of it. They often become so consumed with fear and negative expectations that they even forget that they have the option to look at things differently.

But an optimist develops an awareness of his worry patterns. He notices when they're getting out of control, and he tries to make the conscious choice to intervene on them. An optimist thinks, *What if everything turns out great?* But a pessimist wonders, *What if everything falls apart?*

This becomes a self-fulfilling prophecy that's perpetuated by the pessimist's own energy. As is true of all mental and emotional patterns, your own resonance magnetizes corresponding vibrations from the Universe. A pessimist thinks catastrophically, assuming the worst, grinding out energies of fear and doubt, and inevitably attracting the very results that he feared. It's alarmingly easy to get caught up in this cycle. Worry begets loss, which perpetuates even more anxiety. In this way, fear is an absolute deterrent to the energies of solution and success.

⚛ Optimism produces positive results, perpetuating even more hopeful expectations. An upbeat attitude creates the kind of happiness that carries you through life, even if the results may be a little slow in coming. No matter what's going on, real optimism— the attitude of hope and positive expectation—puts you in the state of Flow, that magical confluence of personal intention and Universal solution.

Which of these attitudes do you tend to embrace? Are you living in fear or in flow? Check the following list to determine whether you tend to be more pessimistic or optimistic.

Pessimist	Optimist
Tends to be fearful and worrisome much of the time.	Feels generally relaxed in the present and trusting in the future.
Sees a negative event as potentially life altering and even irreversible.	Isolates individual problems and sees them as temporary.
Feels powerless, as if he can't handle things.	Looks for manageable solutions and takes action.
Tends to be more nervous, jittery, and uncomfortable.	Tends to be more spontaneous and have more fun.
Tends to be less active and more habitual or addictive.	Tends to be more balanced, active, and social.
Is easily depressed by outside circumstances, and with each new problem the depression gets worse.	May be depressed temporarily, but is more likely to bounce back and move on; determines to let go of the past.

You can easily see how the patterns in the second column would create a more peaceful psychology, but there are many other reasons to choose to embrace this attitude. Studies show that optimistic people are less likely to catch infectious diseases and more likely to recover from them quickly. They also live longer and develop fewer catastrophic illnesses. A recent study of octogenarians showed that the single greatest factor in healthy longevity is the ability to bounce back from loss and defeat and still look forward to the future.

Over and above all the physiological and psychological inducements, there's another—perhaps even more compelling—motivation to become an optimist; that is the energetic and consciousness change it brings to your life. Not only do you become a happier person, but you draw more positive people to you! Assistance from the Universe also manifests in remarkable and surprising ways. From finding a convenient parking spot to getting that dream job, you're far, far more likely to attract the good stuff when you're in the optimistic state of Divine flow.

Getting Past the Pessimist

The choice to become an optimist may not be easy, but it's worth it. Like most important decisions, you don't just make it once, you do so every day. However, it's important enough—and valuable enough—to see that daily action through. No matter how compelled you are to engage in negative thinking, you must use every opportunity to choose a new approach, a fresh attitude that frees you from that mental prison.

If you're lucky, your gloomy outlook is merely a fleeting fear concerning some specific issue that's sensitive for you. But if you're like most pessimists, you can be absolutely addicted to the process of negative anticipation. A lot of people think that if they worry enough, it will help them deal with whatever problem may come up. But being prepared requires planning—not fretting. It's energetically true that *no amount of negative focus can ensure a positive outcome.* So prepare what you need to, but always take aggressive action to cancel out the negativity.

JOURNAL FOR SUCCESS

Whenever worry takes over, remind yourself of the consequences by asking yourself the following questions. Do this often in your journal until it becomes a spontaneous mental process for you.

- What's this negative thought emotionally creating for me?

- Is it really solving any problem?

- Does this thought honor me, increase my sense of self-empowerment, or make me feel better in any way? If not, what new conclusion can I make?

- What kind of energy is this pessimism creating? Do I really want to perpetuate that vibration in my life?

- What kind of results will this resonance produce?

Worrying doesn't protect you in any way. It only makes you miserable in your present and ensures that you'll attract more heartache in the future, so you must aggressively attack your negative tendencies. When you experience a difficult problem or when some cynical conclusion comes up, take some time to write about it.

List the things that you're worried about, and then write some optimistic conclusions to counter those assumptions. At the very least, affirm: *I don't have to make this mean so much. I can let this worry go.* Better yet, affirm: *I am powerful. I believe in my ability to handle anything. Everything is going to turn out fine.*

Affirmation Proclamation

Some people tend to dismiss the use of affirmations, but as you've discovered in the previous chapters, they're a powerful tool in creating both a shift in energy and in consciousness. They're especially helpful in projecting a strong magnetic energy, because the process of affirmation is the conscious intention to draw more optimistic mental conclusions. It counteracts the spontaneous negative thinking that has become a way of life for so many. In fact, chances are high that if you're not purposely engaged in affirmation, you're unconsciously engaged in negation.

This is why it's so vitally important for you to live a more affirmative way of life. It gives you options, shifts both your mental and physical energy, and even creates new neural pathways that can make optimism a more spontaneous reaction for you.

If you're dealing with a difficult issue or an especially destructive belief, practice the technique of affirmation saturation. Shower yourself with positive conclusions that will reverse the pattern; keep repeating your affirmations—even hundreds of times a day—until you feel a shift in attitude. No matter what's going on, it's always a good idea to look in the mirror and affirm: *I value myself. I love myself. I expect the best. I deserve the best today and always.* Then look at yourself and say: *I love you. I believe in you. You deserve to be happy.*

This isn't just the simpleminded repetition of positive but somewhat meaningless statements. Real affirmation is a way of life, a flow of positive intentions and observations that carry you through your day in an optimistic frame of mind. This attitude can help you live with honoring and appreciation, engaging in all of the magnetic energy changes at once.

> ✵ Affirmation is the beginning of change, the begin-
> ning of creating destiny. The Power of Conscious-
> ness decrees: In the beginning—of all things—is the
> word. Make it a positive one.

You can learn to teach yourself new optimistic tricks. Do whatever it takes to silence the voice of your inner enemy, that "evil twin" that can't accept the best. Stop and distract yourself; intervene, let go, and affirm. *Force* yourself to release every one of your pessimistic thoughts by making them neutral at first, and then shift them to be completely optimistic. In time, choosing only positive assumptions will bring unending positive results.

When adversity rears its ugly head, deal with it but never, ever let it define you. Living in pessimism makes *you* your biggest obstacle, as you create conflicted thought and contradictory intentions. If you desire your goal, yet you're pessimistic about the outcome, you're definitely sending the Universe mixed signals. Optimism allows you to move toward your dreams with determination instead of despera-tion. It's the state of unconflicted thought, single-mindedness, and pure intention, and as such, it's a compelling force that the Universe is bound to respond to. When you live with optimism, you achieve optimal results.

✧

AFFIRMATIONS FOR OVERWHELMING OPTIMISM

- *No matter what may be going on, I only choose optimism from now on.*

- *I am relaxed. I am resourceful. I trust in myself and in my future.*

- *I am spontaneous, fun loving, happy, active, and hopeful.*

- *No matter what, I absolutely refuse to fear. Optimism is my new attitude.*

- *I live an affirmative and optimistic life in all that I do, think, and choose. I affirm and acknowledge myself, my value, and my life.*

✦ ✦ ✦

Chapter 16

THE ENERGY OF PURPOSE

The Third Magnetic Energy of Success

---

*"Purpose is something greater than yourself.
It changes who you are into who you are meant to be."*

— Benjamin Earl Taylor, Jr.

Are you living on purpose? Do you have a guiding principle or a central goal that directs your choices and carries you forward? If not, you could be spinning your wheels, spending a lot of time and energy moving in different directions and never really ending up at the destination of your choice.

The difference between being *off* purpose and being *on* is like the difference between a pinball and a bowling ball. Off purpose, you're bounced around from one event to another, blindsided by unexpected occurrences, getting sidetracked into dead-end destinations. Your life is similar to a game of pinball; your energy is scattered, and your results are largely influenced by luck.

Living on purpose, however, makes you more centered and focused and puts you on more of a direct path. Like the game of bowling, your energy and your life are on the straight and narrow, following a more direct course to your goals. Of course, you can always throw some gutter balls as you're fine-tuning your energy game, but eventually a purposeful resonance will score a perfect strike.

What would you say your primary purpose is? Take a moment to think about it now, and if your answer has something to do with work, think again—that's your *professional* purpose. If you believe that it has something to do with your family, you also need to try once more, because that's your *personal* purpose.

Your primary purpose has nothing to do with anything outside of you; it's about your inner life. In your movement from birth to death, there's something greater that must be done—more than acquiring a big house or belonging to a country club, beyond fortune or even fame. It's the only thing that you'll take with you when you leave this life; it's your own personal and spiritual growth.

"Primary" means first or most important, and both of these meanings apply to our spiritual purpose. It's our first motivation for coming to this reality, and it's the most important reason for staying. Clarity of understanding, self-mastery, and deepening love are all part of the process of the spiritual self, the central meaning of our human experience. The wonderful thing is that when these qualities are at the core of your life, it creates a dramatic shift in energy and consciousness, and all of your other goals seem to fall into place.

Only *you* can determine what your spiritual purpose is, although for most, it's about love. Whether it's learning to care for yourself or others, or learning to find a greater passion in your relationship with God and the Universe, love is our greatest education. And once we learn about it, we have to consciously choose it. That's where the Law of Expanding Influence comes in.

The more we release hate and embrace love, the more that positive energy expands in our world—not just for us, but for everyone. Sometimes I go through my day simply repeating this intention as my mantra: *Choose love; choose love; choose love.* If I'm looking critically at myself in the mirror, I let it go and say, "Choose love." If someone cuts me off on my way to work, I release the anger, take a deep breath, and remind myself: *Choose love.* If I'm frustrated with someone at work, I look in that person's direction and simply repeat to myself: *Love, love, love.*

✾ Choosing love as a spiritual purpose isn't just some meaningless, New Age claptrap. It's a powerful energetic choice, a process of switching from a heavy, dense, earthbound vibration to a light, fluid, and beautifully attractive one. As a result, your spiritual purpose can't be entirely separated from your personal or professional ones. The more you work this priority into your life, the more your resonance will sparkle in every arena.

I feel exceedingly fortunate to be able to tie all of my purposes together and make my life's work what I love to do. I feel that my primary—or spiritual—reason for being here is to experience Divine love to the fullest extent possible and then to expand that into the world. As an author, lecturer, and counselor, this has become a big part of my professional purpose as well. And, of course, it's a top priority in my personal life as wife and mother. In recent years, I've also added the mission of being an adoption advocate. This is especially fulfilling, because it brings my intention of love into an issue that's very close to my heart.

There are many people who are striving to find their purpose—whether spiritual, personal, or professional. Part of the problem is a confusion between purpose and motivation. You may be motivated to pay the rent each month, but is this your purpose in life? If you're like most individuals, you're often so driven by your immediate needs, that they—rather than purpose—become the compelling forces of your life.

But in order to align your energies with the Universal Laws, it's very important to determine what your purpose is and then choose to honor it. The most compelling and magnetic meaning that you can bring to your life is one that sparks your passion.

Passion + Purpose = Power

It always surprises me to see how many people fantasize about success without really knowing what specific goal or activity they want to succeed at! So many people tell me that they want to make a lot of money or become famous, yet when I ask them how they're going to do that, they have absolutely no idea. But it's impossible to achieve if you haven't clearly identified your purpose and defined your goal. Without this as your starting point, you won't be focused enough to turn your desire into a reality.

There's a big difference between a dreamer and a doer. The former pictures himself driving a fancy car or flying off to exotic locations, but he actually has no clue about how he's going to make it happen. Unfortunately, big dreams with no purpose only create a vacuum of activity and energy, one where nothing gets done and no real success is achieved.

This is the case for countless people who drift through life resenting their ho-hum jobs yet hoping to win the lottery or inherit a windfall. They envy those who have what they want, and this feeling combined with their own purposelessness only leads to more depressing energy, which actually repulses the very things they're envious of.

The doer understands this pitfall. Unlike the dreamer, he determines for himself what kind of pursuit he's going to engage in. He still has a dream, but he knows what it entails, and he's willing to take all the action necessary to make it come true. Like his aimless counterpart, a doer will also picture himself in that expensive car or jetting around the world, but he builds those images on a steady foundation of personal purpose, planning, activity, and real passion—and that's the energy accelerator. The more ardent the pursuit, the more likely the success.

So how do you find a purpose with passion? Some individuals are fortunate to realize at an early age what kind of path they want to pursue. They're driven by an inner knowing, or perhaps a natural talent. And if they persist, they may find a career where this can be both personally and financially rewarding.

A surprising number of people don't consciously choose their professions, however. Serendipity or circumstance nudges them into their career. I've known many who, having accepted what they thought to be a temporary job at the age of 18, found themselves in the same career 30 years later. If they're really lucky, that path brought them joy and fulfillment.

But many aren't that fortunate when they "fall into" a profession merely by chance. They may think that they're just checking it out, yet they're still there years later, whether they're truly happy or not. They choose to stay due to familiarity, preferring to let go of their dreams in order to maintain the status quo. But this apparent comfort is seductive. It can keep you stuck, even if you're not happy—and it may be especially enticing if you're making enough money to get by. Unfortunately, this combination of income and habit can be a trap.

That trap is fear, and it snaps down around your hopes and imagination like a steel jaw. It slams shut when you find yourself making enough money at something you don't enjoy, yet fearing that you won't be able to equal that sum if you move on to a career you love. *The irony is that you're willing to give up happiness in order to make the money that you think will bring you happiness!* This financial catch-22 can keep people stuck for years, decades, or even their entire lives. They think, *I'll never make it if I try something new. I've been doing this for so long that it's too late to start over now.*

But it's never too late to find a purpose that sparks your passion and pursue something that you enjoy. In fact, it's virtually impossible to achieve genuine success in a field you resent or in a job that you loathe. The resonant frequencies around those kinds of emotions are just too abrasive to attract something joyous to your life.

Passion, on the other hand, is a catalyst for success because it adds the element of excitement, a prime energizer of the Law of Pure Desire. Without that fervor, you can't hope to create the level of excitement necessary to activate the Universal Laws. But with it, your energy of excitement will move you to continued action and spark the energetic fields into wonderful response.

JOURNAL FOR SUCCESS

Here are some tips to help determine your purpose and pinpoint those goals and activities that are most likely to ignite your own personal passion. Take the time to do the following exercise in your journal, and make sure that you consider each item seriously. Remember that your personal and professional purposes are expressions of your individuality. They should resonate with your interests and reflect what you enjoy.

- List some of the things that uniquely make you *you*. Include your personal interests as well as the activities you like to engage in. (For example: interested in politics, enjoy baseball and horseback riding.)

- Now scan that list and write down any hobby, goal, or work activities that can be connected with those interests. If you're unsure, do some research.

- Consider the answers you just gave. Which of these related pursuits do you think can become a professional purpose for you? Which one will excite your passion the most?

For any real satisfaction, your purpose should reflect your own personal values. If it's at odds with your core beliefs, you'll constantly feel off balance—and you may even feel as if you're living a lie. This is absolute poison to your energy, and you can never be truly happy in this state. Keeping that in mind, move on to the following steps.

- List some of the things that you value most. It's fine to include money, but not okay to limit your list to that. Some of these items may have already been included in your earlier list. (For example: time with family and friends, outdoor activities, your religion or spiritual pursuits.)

- What purpose—either personal or professional—will help you prioritize these values?

- What will it take to make this purpose a part of your everyday life?

These are some very important—even life-changing—questions, and they need to be answered honestly if you want to create a *genuine* experience of success in your life. This energy is one of the most magnetic ones for the Law of Pure Desire, because living in alignment with your own personal purpose projects a very dynamic and attractive vibration. In fact, purpose (along with optimism) is the major component of creating a life of passion. This combination is a driving force behind the process of attraction and a primary source of personal satisfaction.

When your purpose aligns with your life work, you get the sensation: *This is who I am. This is what I should be doing.* When you can look at your career path and think in that way, you'll know that in a very important sense, you're already a success.

AFFIRMATIONS FOR A POWERFUL PURPOSE

- *A happy and hopeful life is my purpose.*

- *Every day I look for all the love, understanding, and self-mastery that I can achieve.*

- *I live with passion and personal power. I act on my own behalf each day.*

- *I live with alignment. I stay centered and focused on my goal. I am <u>on</u> purpose.*

- *It is safe for me to follow my bliss. I make choices that honor my spirit.*

⊕ ⊕ ⊕

Chapter 17

THE ENERGY OF PRESENCE

The Fourth Magnetic Energy of Success

"For eternally and always there is only now, one and the same now; the present is the only thing that has no end."

— Erwin Schrödinger

There's an old adage that goes, "Today is a gift; that's why they call it the present." This may sound like just a cute little saying, but it's important to look at the energetic truth of it: *Energetically, we create our reality every moment that we live.* In fact, in terms of our consciousness creation, we never have any other opportunity to do so. That's what makes each second so precious, so much of a gift. The present is our window of opportunity. It opens us to our options of choosing a new approach that will make a difference in our lives. This is the wonderfully magnetic energy of presence: the power to change our future. Every single second is a Universal gift.

But there are so many moments that we just throw away. We're given the blessing of a beautiful sunset, but we're too busy to notice. The Universe offers us another present—perhaps an opportunity to relax—but maybe we're too worried to do so, so we trash that as well. One moment may bring an opportunity to have fun with friends, but we're too distracted by work or other obligations, so we just toss that out, too. What would you do if you kept sending presents to someone who repeatedly threw them away? Of course, you'd stop giving them!

Every moment that we discard is an act of rejection, a brutal dismissal of our own life, and the Universe will respond by dismissing our desires. But if we acknowledge the value of each instant, if we see the beauty, grace, and abundance that's offered there, we'll dramatically change our energy right now and alter the results that we see in our future.

So many of us spend our time elsewhere, worrying about future events and brooding about past difficulties. But what happens when we're continually ruminating about the past or anticipating the future? We lose the potential power of the present. We simply can't take the right kind of mental and emotional energetic action if our minds keep jumping back and forth.

Now Voyager

Oftentimes, we don't have any desire to stay in the present because we simply don't think that it's special enough to be worth our full attention. This approach is just filling time while waiting for something better to come along. We see our lives as an endless series of mediocre and mundane activities sprinkled with only a few truly happy or special events. And while we're waiting for those red-letter days to come along, we live with boredom and disinterest in what's going on around us—or perhaps even resentment and disgust.

This is what I call a layover mentality: deciding that everyday life doesn't warrant enthusiasm or happiness. We're merely on a layover, waiting for some special, but all-too-fleeting, event to lift us temporarily out of our doldrums. Some people never even consider being happy while they're immersed in their daily routine. In the meantime, they'll stay irritable, frustrated, or bored.

Unfortunately, this is how too many individuals look at the world. They're just biding their time until something better comes along. This can become such an ingrained lifestyle pattern that it's possible to go through long stretches—even decades—only seeing life as a burden.

What kind of miserable consciousness does this create, and what kind of reality will come from it? If you're constantly dismissing and devaluing significant periods of your life, you'll only get disregarded and be unappreciated in return. Dismissal of your present is literally creating a consciousness of lack about your very existence!

You must ask yourself: *How often do I feel like I'm just biding my time, just going through the motions?* Whatever activity you're engaged in, you *do* have the option to value your present and create a positive energy there. This choice is where the two magnetic vibrations of appreciation and presence come together to create a brilliant vortex of energy that changes everything from this point forward. This moment isn't just a meaningless layover on the way to something else, it's an actual destination in and of itself—an energetic powerhouse waiting for you to light it up!

> ❈ Every present moment that you arrive at a new perception, a new way of looking at things, you're making a shift in your energy production. And if you choose an honoring, loving, and joyous point of view, you're charging that time with all of your powers at once. No matter what you're doing, you can choose to see value in this instant—even if you're just engaged in a mundane activity, such as driving to work or doing some household chore. This moment is truly special. It's the doorway to the energetic realm and the only time that you're going to have this precise opportunity.

Long ago, I heard a wonderful affirmation by Louise Hay: *The point of power is always in the present moment. . . .* When you study the science of energy and consciousness creation, you can see the absolute truth of these words. There's no solution in the past and no certainty in the future. The only time that you can take any real or energetic action is right now—and filling your minutes with brooding about the past or worry about the future is *not* the kind of action you want to take.

There's a funny saying that goes like this: "If you have one foot in the past and one foot in the future, then all you can do is piss on the present!" Is this really how you want to treat your point of power? When you take care of the present, you don't have to worry about anything else, for when you energize it with value, optimism, and appreciation, the rest will take care of itself—unfolding in seemingly magical ways. Time is the energetic source of your strength, so it's time to take it seriously.

The Universal Laws respond directly to your attitude about your present life. If you can stop worrying about tomorrow and engage in the happiness you seek right now, this will ensure the future you're looking for. So stop waiting for a "special" occurrence to enjoy yourself. The quality of your days doesn't come from extraordinary activities, pleasure seeking, or wish fulfillment. It bubbles up from within, from both your attitude and your intention. You not only need to stay conscious of what you're experiencing, but you also need to *value* it.

Remember that your power of choice puts you in charge of your attitude toward life—whether it's about the present or any other thing. If you find yourself feeling fearful about the future, affirm that you can let it go and choose trust instead. If you're brooding about the past, release that, too, and take back your power in this instant. *Staying present is the ultimate expression of trust; finding joy in the here-and-now is the divining rod to the endless spring of future joy.*

The fact is that anything short of choosing to value this moment ends up destroying the worth of what's to come. So don't spend your life playing the waiting game, thinking that someday soon you'll be happy, but dismissing the chance to choose that now. Take control of your intentions and attitude immediately, and intend to enjoy the present. Bring value and appreciation to the center of your mind and your life. Don't postpone your potential for peace even one moment longer.

JOURNAL FOR SUCCESS

In order to get a handle on your present energy, answer the following questions in your journal. Do this exercise often, especially when you feel as if things are getting out of control.

- What kind of energy have I been creating lately?

- What kind of thoughts and emotions am I engaging in *now?*

- Do I tend to acknowledge the value of my present activities or see them as a burden?

- What are the energetic consequences this could be creating?

- What kind of conclusions can I make in order to see things differently and change my attitude and emotions *now?*

- What can I affirm or appreciate about myself or my experience *right now?*

Are you willing to do whatever it takes to experience real appreciation and happiness today and stop waiting for your life to begin later—maybe much later? *You may not realize it, but this—right now—is the greatest moment of your life.* Now is the moment of creation and opportunity, the energetic seed of all future happiness. You can't go back and make it happen in the past, and you can't leap forward and take action in the future. In fact, the best way to ensure the happy emotions you want to arrive at then is to experience them now.

Use this moment to change your consciousness, energy, intention, action, and attitude, and you'll be doing all that you can to create a brilliant tomorrow. The power of self is found in the simplest moments—every single one of which defines you. You must ask yourself, *What do I choose now? And now?* This is the perfect—and only—time to take control. Don't deceive yourself; you absolutely *can* do it. You already have the power, so give yourself the present!

AFFIRMATIONS FOR A POWERFUL PRESENCE

- *I always take time to see real value in the present moment and opportunity in every present activity.*

- *This very moment creates the energetic momentum of my life. I choose to make it count!*

- *I look for the joy in my life right now and take action to create it in all that I do.*

- *This is a new day—a new opportunity. I can embrace a new attitude right now.*

- *I enjoy the present and trust in the future. I see my life as an adventure that I create every day.*

- *I release the need to worry about the future or relive the past. I focus only on the present from now on.*

⊕ ⊕ ⊕

Chapter 18

THE ENERGY OF APPRECIATION

The Fifth Magnetic Energy of Success

"There is an inherent law of mind that we increase whatever we praise. The whole of creation responds to praise and thankfulness."

— Charles Fillmore

The fourth dynamically magnetic energy is one of the most valuable vibrations in your personal field: appreciation. It's the intention to live with gratitude, the conscious acknowledgment of the value within and around us, the willingness to notice all the good things we already have, and the desire to experience all of life with this attitude. But to really create this vibration, your daily life has to resonate with awareness and gratitude in the here-and-now. This isn't just an idealistic fantasy; it's an energetic necessity, for appreciation is where real pleasure comes from.

The fact is that you can't experience joy without appreciation. Think about the times that you've been happy; recall where you were, what you were doing, and whom you were with. Stop for a moment and let yourself dwell upon those good times now, letting a smile come to your lips and feeling the delight resurface in your heart. As you remember these episodes, ask yourself, *In each situation, what was I appreciating?*

✳ Whether you realize it or not, every single time that you experience happiness, underneath it all you're in the state of appreciation. No matter what it is you're excited about, that feeling means that you're thankful for something. The more you feel that resonance, the more you create a happy life; and according to the Law of Magnetism, your energy of gratitude will only attract more to appreciate in the future.

This is a truly empowering and liberating realization, because you don't have to wait for happiness to come at some vague point in the distant future. You don't have to rely on such things as more money, a new love, a bigger house, or a better job to experience that state of well-being. You can choose to engage in appreciation now. And when you decide to *really feel* it, you will bring bliss to your everyday life.

This is a pivotal point in your energy and consciousness production. You may pursue your goals because you think that they'll make you happy later, but with that attitude, it's impossible to be joyous now. However, when you live by filtering everything through a genuine sense of appreciation, you not only create what you seek right now, you also magnetize increasingly cheerful results in the time to come.

What State Do You Come From?

When we look at our emotional lives, we can see that we tend to bounce around from one state of being to another: happy one day, unhappy the next; excited one moment, worried the next. Our moods are easily shaped by outside circumstances, and most of us are much more sensitive to negative influences than to positive ones. We're often easily frightened, and sometimes the littlest thing annoys us. But what lies beneath these variations?

As you've seen, underneath every emotion of happiness is the mentality of appreciation. And the opposite is true for negative feelings: beneath most them is some sort of dissatisfaction. Which of these mental activities do you engage in most: Do you consciously seek to enjoy yourself in the present and acknowledge what you already have? Or do you look at your life and see everything that's missing? If it's the latter, you need to know that your attitude affects both your consciousness and your energy, and it only perpetuates the dejection you're already feeling.

Some people live in a constant state of dissatisfaction. They grumble their way through life, complaining about what's wrong and focusing on what they lack. It seems that nothing ever pleases them, and unfortunately, their energy makes this sad fact true. *The Universal Laws don't budge on this issue: That which you focus on will expand in your life. And if you're constantly noticing what you lack, then the deficiencies in your life will become overwhelming.*

Your choice to concentrate on what's missing is opting to obsess about the problem instead of the solution. This makes it impossible to establish a consciousness of success; instead you're filtering everything through an awareness of deprivation. Just think of the pieces of your consciousness PIE: The first slice is perception. Identifying lack produces neuropeptides that match the emotion of hopelessness, creating increasing cycles of negative consciousness creation.

The next piece is imagery. The picture of lack is that of a void, a vision of dark emptiness that encourages you to become needy, urgent, and fearful, engaging the difficult forces of the Law of Paradoxical Intent.

For the final piece, examine the quality of your expectation when you tend to see everything through the sensation of scarcity. If that's what you experience, then it's also what you expect—and, of course, it's what you will get.

Some people filter their general dissatisfaction through certain issues. For example, I have numerous clients who've never been satisfied with their weight. One revealed to me that everything in her life—every experience, relationship, and endeavor—has been interpreted through this issue. At the age of 40, she said, "I remember being on perfectly wonderful tropical vacations, but never allowing myself to be happy because I felt that I looked horrible in a bathing suit."

She grieved over all the fun times that she'd lost while worrying about how she looked. She believed that she'd wasted most of her life filtering her experiences through this discontentment. And although she was older and even heavier than before, she then vowed to never let her judgment of her weight stop her from experiencing the real happiness of her life.

Interestingly enough, after she consciously and consistently made this change of mental focus, she began to lose weight far more easily than she'd ever done in the past. The Law of Paradoxical Intent rang true: When she no longer obsessed about it, she was able to lose weight with joy and ease. And although she never became the "skinny" person she'd always longed to be, she finally found herself experiencing a joy that she'd never before allowed herself due to her dissatisfaction with her appearance.

For others, the focusing lens is money and acquisition. It seems that no matter how much they earn, there's never enough. They may drive a nice car, but it's not fancy enough; they may live in a nice home, but it's not big enough. Yet until they choose to be satisfied with what they have, they'll never attract enough to really make them happy.

Unfortunately, many people have an inflated sense of need: They get what they want, and then they crave more. We've become a culture of great wealth, but instead of our riches increasing our appreciation, they seem only to perpetuate our longing. Our level of dissatisfaction increases proportionately to our level of acquisition!

This realization was made dramatically clear to me when I went to Russia to adopt my two children. There, the appreciation level is high simply because the possession level is so low. It's not uncommon for two or even three families to share a small apartment. They have neither the room nor the money to hoard a lot of stuff, so they're grateful for what little they have, and things such as tennis shoes and jeans are prize possessions.

When the adoption agent from Saint Petersburg came to the United States for a visit, she was amazed at the size of everything—the homes, the vehicles, the closets, and people's wardrobes. She was especially amazed by the portions when we went out to eat. She told me once that her family of three could make a sufficient dinner out of the food that was served to one person in one of our typical restaurants.

Can't Get No Satisfaction?

What is this phenomenon of having more and appreciating less? In this wonderfully abundant society of ours, we have so much exposure to so many things that we've become desensitized to the real value in our lives, and we end up needing more to stimulate us. It's like taking a drug every day: Eventually you build up a tolerance, and you need more to create the desired effects. But this isn't the only source of our longing.

Some of us feel compelled to obsess about what we lack because we believe that our negative focus will force us to find a solution. We're always thinking, analyzing, and judging to see if something or someone is valuable enough. But this choice to criticize instead of observe creates a harshness in our energy, a readiness to be dissatisfied—or even annoyed, agitated, or angry. This is what results from the schism between the mind and heart.

Analysis and judgment are functions of the mind, which assigns value, while the heart experiences it. The former looks for problems, but the latter sees solutions. In fact, when we examine our state of dissatisfaction, we can see that *we* are the biggest obstacles to our own happiness. No matter what happens to us, it's what occurs within us—in our minds and thoughts, in our seeking and striving—that causes our greatest misery.

It may seem simplistic, but what would happen if we just quit analyzing and worrying—if we *simply stopped being dissatisfied?* It would turn our need for competition into compassion and our obsession about acquisition into present appreciation. Our energy—and our universal connection—would shift from agitated resistance to willing receptivity.

The consciousness of living from the heart is the key to a spectacular destiny creation. Use your power of letting go to release your dissatisfaction, and harness your power of choice to cultivate your appreciation. Search for things to be grateful for throughout your life and deep within yourself. As you practice consistent and conscious appreciation, you'll not only see dramatic shifts in your daily happiness, you'll also see big changes in the long-term results of your life.

JOURNAL FOR SUCCESS

In order to facilitate this process, I recommend keeping an appreciation and acknowledgment journal. You can keep a separate notebook for this, or you can include it in your success journal.

Every night before you go to bed, jot down a few things that you appreciated that day. Include the big things you have to be grateful for, but also make note of all the little gifts of life, such as the scent of spring lilacs, the sound of birds on a summer morning, or the sparkle of freshly fallen snow in the moonlight. This isn't just some cliché admonishing you to "smell the roses." It's a part of your consciousness and energy production, and your willingness to acknowledge and delight in even the simple things will magnetize joy in great abundance.

Don't limit your appreciation to the outside world. Write down a few items each day that you acknowledge and hold dear about yourself. This process expands the energy of confidence and causes you to see *yourself* as deserving of encouragement. Not only that, it creates a resonance of self-respect, a vibration that will draw back respect and appreciation from others.

It's also a good idea to take some of your favorite things from the appreciation journal and put them on a list that you can refer to whenever you're down and need a lift, or when you're stuck in your head and need to move your consciousness into your heart. There are so many things that can bring gratitude, whether they're beautiful, heartwarming, exciting, or deeply emotional. But when we get lost in the stress of everyday life, we forget all that we have to be thankful for and focus on the negative instead—and this is where the list comes in handy. Use it to remind yourself of all that you have to be grateful for.

I often refer to my own record of thanksgiving. When things get overwhelming, I review it to remind myself of all the wonderful things that I've experienced throughout my life. Some of them are funny little stories about my kids and nephew, and some are beautiful memories of distant travels, skiing, hiking, and white-water rafting.

I remember a time when I was having some difficulty with a seriously depressed client. Our phase entanglement—or connecting energy—really got me down, and I knew that I had to release that energetic influence and move into a heart-centered consciousness. I pulled out my list of appreciation, and just scanning its contents automatically made me happier. But I still went on to look for something specific to give me a lift.

I found a little story that I'd written about my nephew when he was just three years old. I was visiting him one day while he was playing with some toy tools at a little workbench. I asked, "Are you being a builder today?" He said, "Yes," and continued playing for a moment. Then he dropped his little toy hammer and came running over to me. He jumped into my lap, gave me a big hug, and exclaimed, "I love you more than *all* my tools!"

Rereading this anecdote made me laugh, and it completely shifted my focus from worrying about my distraught client to the feelings of happiness that were already present in my heart. It was a simple thing to do, but it brought such dramatic results, creating an immediate emotional and energetic change.

You can fine-tune your appreciation skills by using a technique that I call "Stop, Drop, and Cop." Whenever you're feeling down about something, *Stop* what you're doing. Take a moment to become aware of what you're thinking about, and then *drop* the negativity—whether it's worry, judgment, or dissatisfaction of some kind, say, "I can let this go," and just drop it! Then—wherever you are or whatever you're doing—*cop* an attitude of gratitude right away. Find something you can be thankful for in your environment right now.

If you can't find anything in the present moment, think of something positive from your list, and if you need more help, do the heart-centered process below. The more you practice it, the more easily you'll be able to make this amazing energy shift—even in challenging times.

HEART-CENTERED SHIFT

When you catch yourself worrying about something or when you're annoyed or dissatisfied, use your power of choice to shift your consciousness from the anxiety of your head to the peace of your heart. Take a deep breath, close your eyes, and relax your muscles. Visualize your problem lifting up and floating away like a cloud on the horizon.

Take another deep breath, and as you inhale, sense the energy of your mind quieting down; feel your awareness slowly dropping down into your heart center. Just relax, keep letting go of all concerns, and focus your consciousness on your core.

Then, as you continue to loosen up, let yourself think about something that makes you happy, that you appreciate. Whether it's a bright memory, a person you love, or a beautiful place that you've visited, let yourself picture that now. Visualize all the details, and put yourself right in the center of the picture. Bring it up close, and make it vivid and colorful, immersing yourself in that happy situation.

Feel the joy and let yourself smile. You're so relaxed, happy, and peaceful. This is the state of appreciation, the warm feeling of grateful acceptance. Hold on to it. Know that its ultimate form is loving your life, and when you go back to your daily activities, choose to find gladness and peace in all that you do.

Joyous appreciation is such an important energy that it can't be overemphasized. It brings serenity in the release of striving and allows you to rejoice in what you already have—opening your heart to receiving even more. Every moment spent in this resonance creates a highly attractive vibration and a powerfully creative consciousness. Along with self-honoring, it's one of the most life-changing things that you can do!

I often tell my clients that there's more than one meaning to the word *appreciate*. Of course, the one that you've been learning about in this chapter is "to be grateful for." But when referring to commodities such as real estate, the term means "to increase in value"—which is an absolute energetic truth. Your life will have greater worth when you choose to appreciate it. When you create a real consciousness of the quality of your days, you bring more value there. And choosing to experience joy in the present moment means that your jubilant energy will magnetize much more to enjoy in the future.

⊕

AFFIRMATIONS FOR ENDLESS APPRECIATION

- *I have so much to be grateful for! I look around myself and am satisfied.*

- *I live with joyous gratitude. As I appreciate my life, I attract more and more to appreciate.*

- *I value my life and myself more and more each day. I deserve my own self-appreciation.*

- *I always take responsibility for my own happiness. I find many wonderful things to be happy about each day.*

- *I am choosing to increase my focus on appreciation and self-acknowledgment. I become more and more conscious of all that I have to be thankful for, and I take time to acknowledge it each day.*

⬧ ⬧ ⬧

PART IV

THE FOUR STEPS TO SUCCESS

All of the Universal Laws of Attraction are very real influences in your life, but you need to focus on more than just the energetic and consciousness aspects of your creativity. Serious planning and real action will be required if you want to achieve your desired goals. For many people this is the part of the process that gets the most attention, and yet it's so often misunderstood. It's the technical side of pursuing success, and it takes a profound clarity of intention as well as unfaltering honesty and self-awareness.

The logistics of your process demand an objective approach; you must be able to think clearly about both your desired outcome and what it will take to reach it. While there are many things that you can do to accelerate your progress and enhance the results, there are four steps that absolutely must be followed in order to arrive at your successful destination. They speak to your planning, preparation, and commitment; and they're so intrinsic to the path of success that no real achievement can be attained without them. To become what you seek, your goal must be woven into the fabric of your daily life. It must become your purpose and priority, an ever-present passion that continues to propel you forward.

❖ ❖ ❖

Chapter 19

COMMIT TO YOUR GOAL

The First Step to Success

---

*"Nothing is as necessary for success as the
single-minded pursuit of an objective."*

— Fred Smith, founder of FedEx Corporation

For success to be real, you must make it a part of your life. It's not enough to fantasize about your goal as some distant dream—a hoped-for future event that you may some day get around to. If your plan is to get ahead, you must consciously commit to that. Without paying enough *attention*, your *intention* for it will be empty. In this state, it can't become enough of a force of consciousness to become a reality.

This is a requirement of the Law of Manifestation—for if you want to create something concrete in your life, it must take a real hold in your consciousness first. Your deliberate intention is the link to the creative energy of the Universe, the conduit from thought to reality. If you can't consistently and purposely focus on the pursuit of your goal, then your intentions will falter, wandering off in all sorts of directions, which makes it very difficult to achieve that which you most desire.

A highly focused creative consciousness must have the following three things in order to achieve successful manifestation:

1. **A vivid image and emotional experience of the desired outcome.** You must be able to see the end results clearly, and you must also be able to place yourself squarely in the center of that image with all the accompanying joyous emotions.

2. **A clear understanding of the specific process required to pursue your goal.** You need to know exactly what getting to your desired outcome entails.

3. **A complete willingness to commit to both the process and the goal—whatever that may mean in terms of time, effort, focus, and priority.** This kind of commitment is the determination to prioritize your dream over habits, distractions, fears, addictions, and even immediate gratification.

Life has a way of taking over—often pushing our goals out of the picture entirely. We can easily become distracted by daily necessities and by our own habits and indulgences. Practically anything in our daily routine can become a rut, from when we get up and what we eat for breakfast to what we do after work and how we spend our free time. Eventually, these patterns begin to rule our lives, and many become so deeply indoctrinated that we never even think twice about them.

In this way, we can easily become stuck in a routine; and if it hasn't included our goal from the beginning, we may have difficulty fitting it in. This can be true even when we have a lot of leisure time, because we become accustomed to our patterns of pleasure. We think that we need them to get by, but we may actually be using them to bypass the demands of our goals and desires.

For example, I had a friend who wanted to start his own consulting business. He was stressed at his job, but he didn't want to quit until he got his new business up and running. He'd been in the habit of stopping for a few beers after work and then grabbing some takeout, eating it in front of the television, and falling asleep on the couch.

Since he lived alone, this didn't seem to be a problem—until he had the desire to move on professionally. He knew that he should be using his free time in the evenings to lay the groundwork for his new company, but he was so stuck in his after-work pattern that he couldn't seem to get started. He kept telling himself, *I'll get on it tomorrow,* but each new day was always more of the same.

When he came to me to talk about it, I told him to investigate what really mattered to him and to write a detailed list of reasons for taking action toward his goal. We also created a schedule that slowly moved him out of his routine. He began by giving up the stop at the bar, and he used that time to get his plans started.

Slowly, his enthusiasm about the project increased, and that made it easier to spend more and more time on his goal. He allowed himself one evening a week to follow the old routine, but in time, he didn't even want to do that. He started his own business, and now he loves what he does. He's very successful at it—but he had to give up a deeply ingrained habit to get there.

We often use our habits and addictions as vehicles of escape. Whether we're driven by boredom, stress, anger, or depression, we engage in activities such as eating, drinking, or watching television to distance ourselves from our moods and thoughts. Over time, we tend to assign some very rigid patterns to these temporarily gratifying and distracting activities. We may eat in front of TV, drink after work, or smoke in the car, day after day and year after year, until the force of the habit itself actually becomes the motivation for perpetuating it.

I had a friend who turned an occasional bowl of ice cream before bed into a nightly addiction that he engaged in for years. He paid for it with the loss of productive time and the gain of about 30 pounds! People can become so deeply entrenched in their daily patterns that they find themselves feeling uncomfortable—or even downright anxious—if they have to change. Far from controlling their lives, their habits control them, creating an inertia of energy and consciousness that's absolutely lethal to the process of real achievement.

We fall into this trap because we don't see our everyday actions as conscious choices that have very real consequences. It's easy to get into a rut and difficult to get out of it—especially where our habits and weaknesses are concerned. But remember, we do have the power of choice. Each day at every moment, we have absolute power over the decisions that we make.

There's a fitting story that I once heard about a small town in the remotest regions of northern Alaska. It's a place where winter lasts nearly nine months a year, and the three months of summer are very rainy. This little village is connected to an even more remote one by a single dirt road that becomes heavily tracked with mud in the summer. In the winter, those tracks turn into deep, frozen ruts, making it very difficult to drive. To warn those who are heading out onto this frozen route, there's a sign that says: "Be careful which rut you choose; you'll be in it for the next 40 miles."

Wouldn't it have been wonderful if someone had given us the same kind of warning about the ruts that *we* get into? "Be careful which habit you choose; you'll be in it for the next 40 years!" It could be really easy to just keep doing what you're doing, to move through life letting your accustomed behaviors lead the way. But staying locked into your old patterns has significant energetic consequences—and you'll end up paying the price if you don't let go and choose to commit to your goal instead.

> ❊ More often than not, pursuing an important goal requires greater effort, and success demands even more! It takes extra time, a more dedicated focus, and a greater desire to make your purpose a priority. You must consciously engage your power of choice and actually make your goal a part of your daily habits. Then the action you take, the priorities you set, will become a spontaneous part of both your life and your nature. This is what real commitment is all about.

Whether your goal is to lose weight, paint a masterpiece, own a business, or become a millionaire, it will never happen if you don't consciously commit to making it a priority in your daily life. So it's time to take an honest look at your dedication. Is this really an ongoing priority in your life? If not, are you willing to pay the price of time and effort and make the necessary sacrifices?

JOURNAL FOR SUCCESS

Are you committed to success? Answer the following questions to determine if you have what it takes to achieve—which means a real commitment to your goal. Write your responses in your journal, and reevaluate them periodically to see if you're still on track.

1. What would it take for you to remain consistently committed to making your goal a reality? What would you have to do on a regular basis?

2. What might you have to give up—or at least change in some way—to remain committed to your dream? List the habits that are impediments, and explain what action you need to take in order to alter them.

3. How would you balance this priority with the other important things in your life? Structure a plan that allocates the time spent on all of your priorities.

Your commitment is really a promise to yourself and your future. The energetic consequences of dismissing this important part of your life can be severe, because in essence, you're broadcasting the message that success isn't really important to you. The Universe will receive that message and respond accordingly. But if you choose to make your goal a priority in your life and allow yourself to get excited about its ultimate fulfillment, your passion will muster up support from the world around you. So hold on to your commitment—every step of the way.

✦

AFFIRMATIONS FOR REAL COMMITMENT

- *I intend success. I prioritize my goals every day.*

- *My goal is already taking shape in the energetic realm. I see it clearly; it is a part of my consciousness creation even now.*

- *I am willing to commit to the process, the time, and the effort that my goal requires.*

- *I create balance in my life. I happily include my goals in my daily routine.*

- *I pursue my goal joyfully—for however long it may take.*

⬥ ⬥ ⬥

Chapter 20

SET UP A STEP-BY-STEP PLAN

The Second Step to Success

"To achieve the success of your dreams, you have to live it every day. Success can only happen in small, repeated steps—one step at a time, one day at a time."

— Sharon Anne Klingler, author

Making a specific plan may seem like an obvious part of the process of achievement, but a surprising number of people leave this very important step to chance. They may have some vague notion about how they might be able to approach their goal, but they often don't take it any further than that. This type of casual attitude only encourages procrastination and "future" thinking, both of which will slow you down—or even completely block your desired end results.

✣ A specific plan of action moves you forward, gives you guidelines, and establishes the focus of your conscious energy. According to the Law of Manifestation, everything exists in consciousness first, so if you want the details of your desire to exist in reality, you *must* establish them firmly in your conscious activity before anything else can happen. Your action plan is your mental map to the destination of your desire, so follow it!

I once had a client named Roxanne who was feeling stifled at her secretarial job. She was very artistic, but she didn't know what she wanted to do with her talents; so in her spare time, she tried different activities. One week, she'd focus on writing; another week, it would be painting. Later still, she experimented with jewelry making, pottery, and photography.

Roxanne knew that she wanted to quit her job, but she was all over the place with her options. She found that she was actually quite good at just about everything she tried, and this only perplexed her further. Her energy was far too fragmented to come up with a plan, so we explored her options.

We started by determining what she enjoyed the most, which was jewelry making. We then devised a specific goal and a plan that helped her to stay focused on this one activity. She signed up to participate in a craft show near her home a few months later, so she knew that she'd have to produce the inventory for it. This was exciting, and she spent her evenings and weekends creating beautiful wearable art. Her unusual designs were a big hit, and she signed on for several more shows. Over time, she was making as much in jewelry sales as she had been at her secretarial job, and she was able to move on to doing her art full-time.

Roxanne needed to look at her options objectively. She had to reign in her scattered energy and then create a plan to get going. Once she did that, she became motivated and focused—and her intention to follow through to the end brought her the results that she wanted. Whether you're starting a business or organizing a party, a workable program is the springboard for success.

The following fundamental considerations will help you create both a plan and a clear conscious intention.

1. Know your goal. Just as a map is seldom helpful if you don't know your destination, you'll never be able to move in the direction of success if you don't have a clear picture of your desired goal. You must think long and hard about both what you want and the process of getting there. It helps to write down *all* your options, so use both your intuition and your common sense when considering the alternatives. Be sure of what you want, and consider your talents and lifestyle. Let yourself see all the details of your desired outcome clearly. Without a specific goal, you'll never be able to create a workable plan.

Remember to pick a path that sparks your passion. The more you love what you do, the more your energies will align with the powers of the Universal Laws. This is a lightning rod for synchronicity, that magical place where intention meets reality. The Universe will support your choice to pursue a goal that honors you and represents your heartfelt desires.

2. Find out exactly what it's going to take to reach your goal. There's always a part of the planning process that requires a period of investigation. You may have a general idea of the groundwork necessary to reach the destination you have in mind, but make sure you get some detailed information that you can incorporate into your plan. Talk to people in your chosen field; if possible, try to find someone who's willing to mentor you and give you some sound, ongoing advice.

Do plenty of research. For example, if you want to become a lawyer, surgeon, or licensed psychologist, you'll have to find out what degrees you'll need and which colleges offer them. You'll also have to learn what's required to get into those institutions and how much they cost. If you want to open up a store, you'll need to decide what products you'd like to carry and find out where you can get them wholesale. You should also check out possible locations and investigate the retail history and spending patterns of the area. Every goal requires some prep work, whether it's education, experience, or seed money. Find out what's involved now so that you won't have too many surprises later on.

3. Write down a detailed action plan. Once you find out what your dream will require, you need to put all the steps together so that it makes some sense for you. Draw up a general timeline outlining your desired outcome in terms of the long-term, short-term, and immediate marks that you need to hit. Your long-term goal is the ultimate outcome you're working toward. The short-term ones are the significant steps that get you there, and your immediate missions represent the action that you need to take each day to keep moving forward.

For example, when I'm working on a book, the desired outcome is the finished and edited version. My long-term goal is the rough draft, in the short-term I need the completed chapters, and my immediate objective is always to write, write, write. When I'm working under a deadline, I even try to figure out how much I'd have to produce each day in order to get the project done on time.

In setting up your timeline, you need to be realistic. Things may take longer than you think, or they might go more quickly, but *some* action needs to be taken every step of the way. Write those specific points down and let them become your daily intentions. Having a structured plan will keep your focus from becoming fragmented, and you'll be able to match your action with your intention, the next necessary step to success.

AFFIRMATIONS FOR A PRODUCTIVE PLAN

- *I am willing to lay the necessary groundwork for achieving my desired goal—no matter how extensive that may be.*

- *I know my goal, and I know that I can create a practical plan that I can work on every day.*

- *I set up my long-term, short-term, and immediate goals. I am focused but flexible.*

- *I am creative and resilient. I am open to all the options and abundance that the Universe has to offer.*

- *The Universe supports my plans and intentions for success.*

◈ ◈ ◈

Chapter 21

TAKE ACTION EVERY DAY

The Third Step to Success

"Each of our acts makes a statement as to our purpose."
— Leo Buscaglia

A plan without action is just a fool's daydream. This is where the real work begins, and the positive energy that you create here will be the biggest accelerator to your desired outcome. No matter where you are in your journey, whether at the very beginning or the finish line, there should be at least some action that you can take today to move closer to your goal.

This means that you must be ready to *actively* involve yourself in each part of the process. Are you willing to do whatever it takes? Are you committed to doing the work—be it creative, clerical, sales, managerial, or grunt work—or anything else that your goal may require of you? If you're not set to do the labor, you're not willing to see the success.

This is why it's so important to think your goal all the way through. Some people are great when given direction but can't make the jump to self-motivation, while others are wonderful creators but terrible at marketing—especially when it comes to selling themselves. And many individuals are powerful initiators, yet unfortunately lack the follow-up to see their plan through. But all of the stages of your goal require action. You may be able to delegate parts of it, but ultimately *you* must be responsible for making your dream a reality.

I once saw an interview with the perennially successful novelist Jackie Collins. The interviewer asked what her reaction is to those people who say, "Romance novels are so easy! Anyone could write one." She responded, "Let them!"

It's a breeze to say that something's easy, as long as you're not doing it; the hard part is taking the action and getting it done. You can talk all you want about what you can do—or even what you'd like to do—but until you actually *do* it, that's just hot air. So stop giving lip service to your plans, and start taking the consistent action necessary to make your goal a reality. But in order to prioritize the kind of time and effort this will take, your goal must be important to you—at least as significant as the other time-consuming requirements of your life.

People often confuse the issues of importance and immediacy. They think that if something needs to be done right away, it must be more important than what can be easily put off. Having a lot of tasks that need to be done (even mundane chores) can give you feelings of immediacy and even urgency—which can unfortunately be misinterpreted. The laundry and the dishes may need to be done, but are they really more important than working on your goal?

If you allow all the little tasks of life to become your priority, you'll never set aside enough time to consistently work on what really matters. You could go from morning to night taking care of your daily business without ever giving a single thought to your goal. And when you throw in endless distractions and mind-numbing indulgences, you can completely lose sight of the dream.

⚖ Keep the Universal Laws in mind! Today's action (or inaction) is an energetic cause. Since every effort expands your intention in the energetic realm, no activity toward your goal should ever be considered a waste of time. All that you do broadcasts your vibration and focuses your consciousness creation, so *do* something different—something meaningful—now.

It's time to create balance in your life and set your priorities in a way that will reflect what's *really* important to you. If your dream is worth achieving, then it's worth taking daily action! Even if you have a long-term goal that seems very far away, don't put off the preparation. Take some action today. Even if you feel you've completed much of the work, don't stop now. There may still be something that can move you forward.

TIPS FOR TAKING ACTION

Review the following pointers often, and keep going until you reach your ultimate outcome.

- **Clearly define the action needed for each step of your plan.** Create specific intentions for each immediate and short-term goal within the long-term timeline.

- **Make a list of *all* the reasons why you want your desire to become a reality.** Write down every wonderful thing that it would bring to your life. Then, when you find it difficult to get excited about the work you have to do, read your list. It will inspire new energy and renewed determination.

- **Structure some kind of action into your daily schedule.** If you can, try to book it at the same time each day, when you know you'll be focusing solely on your goal, yet keeping in mind your personal energy patterns. If you know that your energy fizzles out in the afternoon or evening, don't place your most important tasks there.

- **Review your daily action plan at least once a week.** Reevaluate it as you complete each task, and be flexible. Give yourself more time when you need it, but if you do get done with a short-term goal earlier than expected, move on to the next item on your list.

- **Create a priority list.** Carry it with you and add to it if you get some new ideas. Check off each item as it gets completed.

- **When confronted with obstacles or distractions, reread your personal intentions—all of them.** Remember the success intentions you wrote down at the beginning of your journal? Turn to them when you need to rekindle your motivation. If you haven't yet written those down, do so now. They'll help focus your consciousness on your long-term goal.

- **Take some time each morning to visualize** *today's* **action.** Picture in detail when and where you're going to do what you need to, and see yourself engaging in the activity with enjoyment. At the end of the day, visualize the happy completion of some specific activities yet to come.

- **Repeatedly envision your desired end results, and let that image spur you on to even more action and excited intention.** Keep the picture of your goal front and center in your life. Feel it, desire it, and get excited about it! Affirm that you're attracting the outcome you desire even now. This will align your action with the dynamic forces of Universal intention, accelerating your achievement of success.

⊕

AFFIRMATIONS FOR SUCCESSFUL ACTION

- *Today's action creates tomorrow's results. I choose to take action now.*

- *I am willing to do whatever it takes to see my goal through.*

- *My goal is important enough to work on every day. Action turns my desires into reality.*

- *Each morning, I visualize what I'm going to do that day. I see it, and I make it a priority.*

- *I am always patient and persistent. Every day, I take action in the direction of my own goals. I know that my dreams and desires are already taking shape in the energetic realm.*

◈ ◈ ◈

Chapter 22

LET GO OF ATTACHMENT WITHOUT STOPPING THE ACTION

The Fourth Step to Success

"Relinquish your attachment to the known, step into the unknown, and you will step into the field of all possibilities."

— Deepak Chopra

For some people, this is the most difficult step to understand, because they become very attached to their goals. They often think that this will motivate them to persevere, and they fear that letting go will cause them to give up, but just the opposite is true. The more needy you are about your goal, the more your desperation will make you miserable, sabotaging your success and killing your motivation to persevere.

Your persistent action starts with your attitude, not your attachment: Are you determined or desperate? Determination is an approach of *calm but continuous action.* It allows you to concentrate all your effort into creative productivity instead of emotional unrest. This resonance is centered, certain, and focused—and it produces results!

Desperation, on the other hand, moves you out of focused action into emotional *re*action. It causes you to linger in fear and apprehension, a consciousness that blocks both action and creativity. This endless agitation eats up your energy and requires even more effort. And when you project a desperate vibration into the energetic realm, it can only create that kind of reality. So as difficult as it may seem, you must let go of the feeling of desperation.

Thoughts such as *I can't be happy without this* or *I'll never be a success without that* only make you miserable, while broadcasting very ugly signals of longing and need. They absolutely ruin your energy of presence, because they conclude that you can't be happy or successful now. Your desires will be repulsed by this vibration, and your negative results will only lead you further into desperation. Your fear that you can't be happy will become a prophecy fulfilled.

※ You must let go of the urgency and set adrift any thought that attaches your potential for happiness to the achievement of any external thing. Release desperation by defining your goal as something that enhances, rather than completes, your life. Be patient and trust in the Divine timeline. You'll attract what you desire when you trust, let go, and choose to create joy each day.

Your Daily Dose of Vitamin E

Your success is a big commitment, because to get where you want to go, you need to maintain a high level of energy, one that will accelerate the productive times and stimulate you when it's slow. You can maintain this high energy with a daily dose of excitement, which I refer to as "vitamin E." This attitude is the fuel of your intention; it's motivating and invigorating, and it needs to be renewed every day. To do this, affirm your belief and visualize your goal achieved. Smile and feel your enthusiasm moving through you. This activity isn't just silly daydreaming; it stimulates brain chemistry and focuses consciousness creation. But your attitude of excitement shouldn't be limited to your goal. It must also be applied to your everyday life and to all the actions that your goal requires.

This is a problem for a friend of mine who's always wanted to write the "great American novel." She's extremely witty, eloquent, and urbane, and can easily see herself as a best-selling author, going on the talk shows and wowing everyone with her literary genius. There's only one problem: She hates to write!

Whether she lacks the self-discipline or just can't muster up enough interest in the process itself, she's never been able to compose anything of length or substance. She still talks about the novel that's in her computer, but until she can create some real enthusiasm for each step of the journey, she's never going to make that particular dream come true.

This is the key to staying active yet unattached: Get excited about the process itself! You may be thrilled by the image of your successful outcome, but can you engender the same buzz when you see yourself doing the work that it takes to get there? If you visualize yourself winning a marathon, can you also imagine yourself training hour after hour, day after day, repeatedly pushing through exhaustion and pain? If you can envision yourself being promoted to vice president of your company, are you geared up to put in the overtime hours and take the risks that others may be afraid of? If you dream of acting on a hit television show, are you also willing to take acting lessons and show up at cattle calls with hundreds of other hopefuls, praying for that callback but willing to deal with the rejection?

And if, indeed, you're capable of seeing yourself engaged in all of the arduous tasks involved in the process, can you then take it even one step further? Can you see yourself *enjoying* the work and doing it for its own sake? In other words, would you still get excited about it if there were no fame or fortune at the end? This is what the Law of Pure Desire is all about. When you find the process itself engaging, you bring your life energy to it every day. Picture yourself happily engaged in the action of your goal, and *then* picture the happy outcome, too. Hold these images in your heart and mind, and let them be your guides.

TIPS FOR TAKING ACTION WHILE LETTING GO OF ATTACHMENT

There are several things that you can do to move out of a desperate orientation into a happy and active pursuit of success.

- **Tune out all negative thinking.** Whenever you notice yourself in an unpleasant energy state, change the stations on your cognitive radio. Imagine yourself pressing the "seek" button on your thoughts, and keep going until you find a thought that resonates with the higher vibrations of trust and determination. Let all else go, because negative thinking will never produce positive results.

- **Interrupt all negative emotions.** When you're feeling down, you can completely bypass your thoughts by consciously intending a different emotion. This time, push the "seek" button on your emotional radio. Look for the images, memories, and positive expectations that you associate with a happier state. Breathe, smile, and shift your focus as you choose peace of mind instead of worry and doubt.

- **See the value in your process.** Whatever action you're engaged in—whether you're taking classes or putting in overtime—never view the path to your success as a burden. Be willing to engage in the process for its own sake. Look for pleasure and joy in all that may be required to reach your goal.

- **Affirm yourself, your future, and your worthiness several times a day.** Acknowledge your resourcefulness, strengths, and capabilities, and always know that you deserve the very best.

- **In all of your actions and decisions, maintain your honor and dignity.** No matter what may happen, never lose sight of this guiding principle. Success that costs you your dignity is not an achievement, but rather, profound personal failure.

- **Keep working on your confidence.** It isn't possible to be happy, active, or successful when you're always down on yourself, so get rid of the doubt and self-criticism. Believe in yourself and your ability to make your own dreams come true—and determine to keep taking action until they become a reality.

- **Start to notice all of the many ways that you're already a success.** Congratulate yourself on the value that you've created in your life—and on the gifts that you bring to the world. Decide to make your biggest success the mastery over your own energy and consciousness. Then, every other achievement will follow.

- **Learn how *not* to be *un*happy.** Self-love and optimism are the mental foundations for real joy. If you have trouble being happy, look at how you feel about yourself and what your general outlook on life tends to be. Choose to release the thoughts that make you miserable

- **Laugh and smile more, even when you may not feel so inclined.** Smile every day and envision your desires as already achieved. This combination of joy and visualization changes your chemistry, consciousness, energy, and results!

- **Be the person you want to become—right now!** How would you feel if all your dreams came true? Would you be more joyous, playful, and loving? Choose to be all that and even more, beginning today.

Your personal energy ignites the beacon of your truth for all the world to see. It's the vibration of your inner light that creates the real image you send out. If you feel that you've been dimmed by disappointment or urgent desperation, it's time to change all that and quite literally take "charge."

Charge your energy with excitement and imbue your intention with the sparks of purpose and determined action. At every opportunity, alternate your current from lack to have, from pessimism to optimism, and from doubt to self-trust. Every single choice to switch these vibrations creates another positive impulse and shines a brighter beam throughout the world, accelerating your success with unattached enthusiasm and joy. When you connect a genuinely joyous effort with the image of your successful completion, your intention will be driven, your energy will be brilliant, and your action will bring results!

AFFIRMATIONS FOR UNATTACHED ACTION

- *Every day I take calm but continuous action. I remain determined, peaceful, and directed.*

- *I release urgency and live with patience. I take action with calm certainty.*

- *I pursue my goal with open receptivity. I am always willing to receive.*

- *I engage in each action for its own sake. I see purpose in the process.*

- *I bring delight to the effort no matter what the outcome. I live with joy.*

⊕　⊕　⊕

PART V

THE THREE UNSEEN ASSISTANTS TO SUCCESS

It's undeniably clear that energy is a fundamental part of the workings of the Universe. Countless unseen forces move within and around us, impacting our experience of life itself. But in addition to the vibrational forces we've already talked about, there are three unseen assistants that abide solely in the energetic realm. They're the vibrations of the spirit, and their energy is so powerful that it would be a serious mistake to ignore their help.

Spiritual energy moves through all creation. In fact, it's the most dynamic force of both the natural and preternatural worlds—and it's capable of unlimited accomplishment. Consciously connecting with this unfathomable power is the single most important thing that we can do with our lives, yet it's so often the least prioritized. Even the spiritual part of our own identity is easily dismissed—mostly because it just doesn't seem as important as our physical or material needs. We're so busy trying to make money in order to be happy that we disregard one of the most profound sources of contentment available to us!

The world of spirit is filled with abundant joy and unlimited resources. Its energy is both local and nonlocal, individual and Universal, present and infinite. Each being—including you—has a specific identity, yet can't be separated from any other individual, or even from the source and flow of all creation.

These are all very heady concepts, but they must be considered, because this spiritual vibration is where the "magic" comes from. When you connect with this overwhelming Universal force, you attach yourself to the source of all things wonderful. In the joy of this brilliant connection, you create miracles, and you realize that you are one yourself! In fact, the ethereal and physical realms are spectacular beyond our comprehension; and when you resonate at the level of the spirit, your vibrations open your life to all that is beautiful, bountiful, and joyous.

◈ ◈ ◈

Chapter 23

YOUR HIGHER SELF

The First Unseen Assistant to Success

---

*"The Source is unlimited. It knows no boundaries;
it's endlessly expansive, and endlessly abundant. . . .
Discarding doubt is a decision to reconnect to your original self."*

— Dr. Wayne W. Dyer

The spirit world provides us with wonderful energies that have the highest intentions and the power to assist us in achieving our goals—and the closest and most immediate of these helpers is actually yourself! This identity is your soul or your higher self. (It's not "higher" because it floats above you or is somehow better than the rest of you; it's called this because it vibrates at a higher frequency than your physical self does.) You forge your connection to both the Divine presence and the great abundance it can bring through your soul, and this is also how you can access all the information, power, and resources that you'll ever need.

❊ Your spiritual self knows that its essence, and very existence, is unlimited and eternal. It realizes that its expression doesn't end with this life, which is but a fleeting whisper of thought in the long and glorious journey of being. The realization of this truth brings a pervasive sense of calm and safety to your everyday experience, one that transcends your perceptions of limited time and restricted opportunity. Your own spirit opens you to the infinite and unlimited reality that is present even in the here-and-now.

Without this eternal definition, time is your enemy. You may become desperate, anxious, and controlling—with fear as the electrical undercurrent of your life. This energy fills your personal pursuits with an urgency that sabotages the very happiness you seek. But embracing your timelessness radically changes your human experience of fear, integrating a broader, more peaceful approach to everything—including your goals.

Higher Self, Higher Powers

Your higher self is actually more aware of what you need than you are. It has all the solutions that you seek, and access to great fields of information anytime you desire. It's also capable of any strength you'll ever need, but you must open yourself to receiving its power. When in doubt, ask it to bring you the trust and peacefulness that comes from releasing worry. If you're confused about your options, ask your higher self for the wisdom to know just what to do—and for the courage to follow through.

Every personal characteristic is available through these vibrations. Attributes such as confidence, wisdom, courage, determination, love, and hope are all within your spirit self. And even if you feel as if you've never experienced some of these before, your eternal soul has. It's willing to bring them to you whenever you need them—in any situation, at any time.

POWER MEDITATION

To bring any particular quality to your physical and mental experience, relax and visualize a beautiful light shining in your heart center. See the glow and feel the warmth of this beautiful brilliance. Know that this radiance is your true and highest self, capable of providing any quality you desire. Whether it's grace, compassion, persistence, discipline, peace, purpose, dignity, or anything else, name it and call for it from your eternal core. Just say the word, breathe deeply, and allow yourself to relax and feel that particular energy filling you up.

Try this now: Take a deep, cleansing breath and say "Confidence." Call for the feeling from deep within your heart and soul. Breathe again and relax into the sensation, meditating on it as you continue to repeat the name of this wonderful quality. Feel it vibrating in your heart and mind. Experience the energy of confidence growing within, filling you, lifting you up, and making you strong, certain, and free.

Allow yourself to do this process with any strength you desire to experience. Relax, repeat the name of the characteristic you desire, and relive the feeling—and soon it will be fully yours.

In addition to this simple technique, there's also a wonderful affirmation that's taught by a friend of mine who's a truly inspiring counselor and lecturer in Lily Dale, New York. At his seminars, Tom Cratsley encourages people to tap in to their souls' magnificent powers by using affirmations that start with the phrase *I open myself to my spirit's capacity. . . .* They end with a specific intention to change, heal, or receive—whatever may be needed at the time.

This is a dynamic way to connect with your own inner strength. No matter what it is that you have to do, you can use this intention to achieve it. To begin, relax and breathe deeply; then meditate on your heart center and feel your power growing there. As you do, consider the issue you're dealing with and affirm your specific spiritual focus.

Use it for anything you need. For example, you could affirm: *I open myself to my spirit's capacity . . .*

- *. . . to trust*
- *. . . to release worry*
- *. . . to forgive myself*
- *. . . to receive information*
- *. . . to finish this project*
- *. . . to wake up refreshed*
- *. . . to take risks*
- *. . . to be peaceful*

You can rely upon this powerful technique whenever the need may arise. It reminds you that you have unending options in personal strengths, positive emotions, and creative intentions—so use them!

Dignity of the spirit is every bit as much a part of the human experience as fear or worry. In fact, your higher self is the part of you that feels no fear and knows no boundaries. It's your soul's identity that brings unending resourcefulness to your life. In addition to all the energetic states you'll ever need, this aspect has access to all the wisdom of the infinite and eternal Universe.

You're one with the Divine mind, and this source of all knowledge is available to you even now. Your essential self is a wellspring of information, so ask your questions, quiet your mind, meditate, and listen to your intuitive response. Whenever you need to make a decision or get clarity about something, request the information and ready yourself for the answers that you'll certainly receive.

Becoming Inspired

What happens when you define yourself according to the expansiveness of your soul instead of the limits of your body and mind? It opens you to Universal inspirations. There are countless cases of people who've been truly inspired at unexpected times. The fields of science, art, literature, and even finance are filled with stories of apparent miracles. These moments are energetic responses that come at a time when the higher self resonates with the spirit of the Universe. In fact, the very word *inspire* means to be "in spirit."

This isn't necessarily a mystical process, although it may seem that way. The cosmos is actually filled with information and boundless creativity. Like the morphogenetic fields that carry the energy of emotion, great fields of data also carry the eternal wisdom and knowledge of all ages—past, present, and future. This is always available through your resonant connection with the Universal flow. The only thing that stops you from tapping in to it is your own resistance. Obstacles may come in the form of doubt and distractions, but once you let these energy blocks go, you'll find the answers that you seek coming to you in truly unexpected and mystical ways!

I believe this synchronicity with the Divine mind is the source of countless inventions, discoveries, and even great works of art, music, and literature. One particularly astounding inspiration happened to California chemist Kary Mullis, when he invented the polymerase chain reaction (PCR), arguably one of the most important breakthroughs in understanding and decoding DNA.

In his book, *Dancing Naked in the Mind Field,* Mullis tells the story of how he'd been working in the lab trying to find a solution to DNA identification with no luck. One day he left the lab and drove to his cabin in Anderson Valley, California. Looking up at the hills and the blossoms of the buckeye trees, the solution suddenly became clear to him. In a split second he was inspired with the answer, and he pulled over to write it out.

He continued working when he got back to the lab, but the original solution was a bolt of inspiration. He later said it was so simple that he couldn't understand why no one had come up with it before. But the information had been locked up in the morphogenetic fields, waiting for his matching resonance to tune in to it and take it away.

Mullis had been truly inspired. The answer hadn't revealed itself in the lab, while he was poring over his notes. It came to him as he was driving his convertible, blissfully looking at the beautiful trees dotting the hillsides. He'd been seeking the answer, and he was relaxed and open to receiving. It was all there waiting for him, and his desire and intention moved the information from the energetic realm into his reality.

This revelation brought him the Nobel Prize, and its influence has spread throughout the world. The process that resulted from his discovery has totally shifted the understanding of DNA, helping predict and save people from genetically predisposed diseases and radically changing forensic criminology.

Mullis isn't alone in this type of experience. Writers, artists, inventors, and people from all walks of life throughout all periods of time have experienced the magic of spontaneous inspiration. Einstein often said that his greatest solutions came at times when he wasn't thinking about the problems. Thomas Edison kept a cot in his laboratory, and he reported that he frequently got the answer he was looking for upon waking from a nap. You can get inspired, too, if you simply relax, open up, and ask.

LET YOUR HIGHER SELF DO THE WORK

One way to tap in to this amazing power is to get more and more comfortable with tuning in to your intuition. To do that, you need to quiet your mind and listen for answers; then you've got to be willing to recognize and follow the guidance that you get. Learn to listen to your gut feeling more often, and start to distinguish the difference between the voice of intuition and that of fear. Sometimes they can sound so similar that you have to go deep within and listen to your heart to know the difference.

I once met a woman who was scheduled to be on the airplane that was blown up over Lockerbie, Scotland. She'd felt compelled to delay her departure by just a few hours, yet another part of her hesitated to pay the extra money for rescheduling. But she listened to her higher self, and let go of the monetary fear. She spent the extra cash, and her intuition saved her life.

> To increase your intuitive connection with the Universal flow, calm your energy and release your concerns. Learn how to relax and let go of all the hurry and worry you may be feeling. These are the vibrations that throw you off your spiritual connection. Regular meditation and peaceful reflection will connect you to a higher source and move you into the peaceful current of Universal love, guidance, and information.

Whenever you're in need, think about the issue you're working on and ask your higher self for help. When you go to bed at night, send your spirit out into the world to do your work for you. Whether it's convincing someone of the efficacy of your ideas or just getting you the specific information that you need to proceed with your goal, your higher self has more power than you know.

As you fall asleep, direct it to move out into the Universe on your behalf. Keep a notebook by your bed so that you can write down any impressions that you may have during the evening. Even your dreams may have the answers you seek, so jot them down and remain open to seeing the truth within.

The spirit energy that's always with you is a part of both your present and eternal definition. You'll never be more in spirit than you already are right now. Your soul doesn't get greater, more powerful, or wiser when it's released from your physical body; it just becomes less encumbered with material distractions. Right now, your essence has the power to tap in to the fields where all wisdom is stored, and it can connect with all the energetic realms. So ask your higher self for help, but don't stop there. Send your request out into the world—you may be surprised by the responses you get!

⊕

AFFIRMATIONS FOR CONNECTING WITH MY HIGHER SELF

- *Every day I am becoming more and more aware of my own eternal spirit. I live in the peace my spirit brings.*

- *I am open to my own spirit's clarity, wisdom, grace, and power.*

- *I open myself to my spirit's capacity to love and be loved, to create, to trust, and to receive.*

- *More and more, I am listening to my intuitive voice. Inspiration comes in many ways and at unexpected times, bringing knowledge and guidance each day.*

- *I release worldly concerns and embrace the peace of my eternal identity.*

◈ ◈ ◈

Chapter 24

ANGELS, GUIDES, AND LOVING SPIRITS

The Second Unseen Assistants to Success

---

*"Outside the open window
The morning air is all awash with angels."*

— Richard Wilbur

The spirit world is wider and more populated than most people could ever imagine. In addition to the energy of your own soul, the energy of every other individual pulsates through time and space. There are unseen entities smiling upon you, willing to assist you in a myriad of ways. These beings, including angels, guides, loved ones, and other caring hearts of the energetic realms, are always vibrating their messages of love and assurance in your direction.

Angels

Throughout time and in pretty much every religion, angels have been believed to be the servants of God and the helpers of humankind. Don't dismiss this astounding power because you feel that it's just too religious or weird. If there's something you want to do or achieve, call on the angels for help. As with all kinds of assistance—spiritual or otherwise—you have to ask in order to receive.

There are many stories of angelic presence in all sorts of situations. A friend of mine who works in a somewhat hazardous factory job told me that he asks the angels to protect him whenever he goes to work. One day a fire broke out, and the smoke was so thick that he couldn't find his way to the exit. He heard someone call out his name and followed the voice to the door. When he got there, however, there was no one to be seen.

An Olympic ice-skater I met told me that she calls upon the angels all the time. She often feels them dancing with her on the ice, even lifting her up when she performs her jumps. Another friend who's a pilot for a small commuter airline once found himself in the middle of a huge storm over Lake Superior. His 12-passenger plane went into a nosedive, and although he tried with all his might, he couldn't seem to pull the aircraft out of it. He prayed for assistance and suddenly felt two strong arms helping him bring up the nose of the plane, allowing him to finish the flight and get his passengers safely to their destination.

These people asked for help from their angels, and they certainly got it. But assistance from the spirit world isn't limited to the angelic realm.

Guides

Put your requests out there, because there are countless guides who are willing to help. These assistants may be saints or other spiritual masters. Comedian Danny Thomas learned this firsthand, and his one request ended up saving thousands of lives.

In the early 1940s, Thomas was having a great deal of difficulty trying to make it in the entertainment business. He'd done some radio work and stand-up comedy, but he wasn't making enough money to support his young family. His wife wanted him to leave the entertainment industry and become a grocery clerk. She was pregnant, and they were so poor that he thought this might be his only option.

He'd heard about St. Jude—the patron saint of hopeless causes—so he went to the local church and prayed to the holy man. Thomas asked for a sign about whether he should stay in entertainment or go into something "more stable," and he decided that if nothing happened with his comedy soon, he'd get a regular job.

Soon after that, he had a dream about going to Chicago. He listened to that inspiration, and on his first day in Chicago, he was cast in several parts on radio shows. Later he went on to have two hit television series. He also founded a very successful production company that created many popular shows and brought him great wealth.

When Danny Thomas asked for St. Jude's intercession, he said that he would build a shrine in the saint's name to thank him—and he did much more than that. In 1962, he founded the St. Jude Children's Research Hospital where treatment is given to kids with catastrophic illnesses. Started under the auspices of Danny Thomas's personal funding, the policy was created that no child would ever be turned away due to a parent's inability to pay.

This amazing place is now on the leading edge of childhood-disease research, and in the decades since its founding, many thousands of young lives have been saved. The spiritual help that Danny Thomas sought from St. Jude so long ago is now bringing answers to the prayers of families from all over the country. He was awarded the Congressional Gold Medal for his humanitarian endeavors.

I have a guide I often turn to, also. St. Anthony is the patron of lost things, and you can call upon him to find anything you've misplaced. There's an invocation that goes, "Dear St. Anthony, come around. Something's lost and can't be found." Say this out loud while thinking of the missing item, and you should soon get an idea that leads you right to what you're looking for.

I turn to St. Anthony all the time, not just for lost items, but also for assistance in locating information or support. I even asked him to help find our adoptive children and bring them home. Over the years, I've called on St. Anthony so often that now I just call him Tony!

A few years ago, I was giving a lecture to a rather large audience, talking about spirit assistance and telling a few stories of how St. Anthony has helped me. When I gave the invocation, a lot of people wrote it down, but one woman in particular went running out the back of the room. I finished my lecture, and upon leaving the hall, this same person came up to me. She apologized for leaving, and told me that she had to call her sister right away to tell her about St. Anthony.

The woman's sister had lost their grandmother's engagement ring, which was not only an expensive antique, it was also very dear to them both. She recited the invocation over the phone, and then they both said it out loud together. Immediately, her sister got an image of a drawer in her dresser. She opened it—and the ring was sitting right on top! She couldn't understand it, because she'd looked there a dozen times before, and once had even dumped the contents out onto the bed. In addition, she'd just gotten some socks out of the drawer that morning, and the ring hadn't been there.

The woman concluded her story by saying, "I'm so surprised!" I told her that I hear that kind of story all the time, and it wasn't so astonishing, because St. Anthony is a loving, supportive soul. She answered, "Oh, it's not that. I'm surprised because we're Jewish!"

Rest assured that the spirit world is nondenominational. I talk to everyone from the Holy Spirit to Sai Baba to my beloved grandmother Anna. You can ask for help from anyone, too, calling upon saints, the Buddha, prophets, angels, or any of your loved ones.

Loved Ones and Other Spirits

There's a well-known story about Enrico Fermi, the acclaimed physicist. At a very early age, he and his brother Giulio studied physics with a passion. Tragically, Giulio died when Enrico was about ten years old. After this loss, Enrico threw himself into reading physics books of all kinds. Toward the end of one volume, his sister noticed something peculiar about it. She asked him how—at the age of 11—he could understand a book that was written entirely in Latin. He told her that he understood everything in it, and he hadn't even noticed that it was in a language completely unfamiliar to him.

Some people who know the story say that it was Enrico's deceased brother who translated the work for him. Others believe that he was helped by an angel, while there are those who are convinced that he simply had an inner knowing. Whatever the source of his miraculous comprehension, he used it to become a leader in nuclear and radio-active science at a very early age.

Don't be afraid to ask for help from all possible sources. Request answers and success! It's well known that Cornelius Vanderbilt consulted a spiritualist for advice on business investments. He went on to amass a fortune and founded a university.

Wherever the aid may have come from, all these stories have one thing in common: The assistance that was needed didn't originate in the mundane, physical world. It came from the energetic realm that's home to the unseen places and loving personalities who have our best interests at heart. Our angels, guides, and guardians move freely in—and have influence over—both the physical and energetic worlds. There's astounding information and assistance vibrating all around you. In a world of pure potential, all that you'll ever need is right at the edge of consciousness, waiting for you to open the door.

AFFIRMATIONS FOR CONNECTING WITH LOVING SPIRIT ENERGY

- *Loving assistance comes my way. I am open and grateful.*

- *Angels grace my life with kindness and compassion.*
  I am protected and well cared for.

- *Whenever I have a question or problem, all I have to do is ask.*
  I always receive the answers I need, and I am grateful.

- *Prayer brings power and purpose to my life. I pray with ease*
  and peacefulness.

- *The Universe is filled with loving intentions. I now align my own*
  loving intention with that abundant flow.

⊕　⊕　⊕

Chapter 25

THE DIVINE PRESENCE

The Third Unseen Assistant to Success

"We are so filled with trouble that the Divine Melody is never heard. If we could see . . . if we could understand, if we only realized the presence of the All, what could we not do?"

— Ernest Holmes

The Divine source of all creation exists in every wave and particle of the cosmos. This compelling energy is the heartbeat of life and the birth of all things—including every success. As such, that Presence needs to become a real and viable part of your life. If you dismiss this amazing force, your dreams may die merely from spiritual starvation. But if you see the Divine as a giver of life and co-creator of your existence, you'll forge your energies with unlimited power and create a consciousness of peace and tranquility that permeates your entire existence.

This shouldn't be just some idealistic task, but rather a heartfelt experience, a process where you ask for and receive God's loving influence every day. The personal dignity inherent in human life comes from the soul's origin, and it reveals the real nature of our eternal truth. This connection transcends all problems, lack, and worry. It brings a greater sense of peace and constancy, one that always draws you back to your source and your solution.

To arrive at this peaceful place, you must define yourself as spirit first. In this definition, your worth isn't based on externals, but on your Divine legacy. You're holy and so is your life. To tear yourself down rejects your sacred identity, which is the real source of personal success. You must see your value and the worth of your eternal life, finally letting go of judgment and conditional self-acceptance, because such material measures consistently deny the innate holiness of your human self. The living presence of the Divine within is your ultimate source of worthiness, and when you embrace this truth, the world will enfold you in its blessings.

In this way, your spiritual and personal success are intrinsically linked to your self-regard. You're a child of God, a manifestation of that eternal love and light, and how you treat yourself is a statement to God about your capacity to love one of His children. Would you let someone talk to your child the way that you've been speaking to yourself? When you criticize yourself, God is asking you, "How could you treat My beloved one this way?" Your judgment denies the eternal spirit of your life, and if self-loathing and self-condemnation are allowed to continue, they'll wall up the light within you until your magnetic energy is as dense and dark as a distant black hole.

You can't separate who you are from who *You* are. If the Divine presence isn't integrated into how you truly feel about yourself, then the most attractive vibration of the Universe will be blocked within. This is the major malady of humankind: All over the world, millions of people feel their vital source energy dammed up in their own broken hearts. It's a painful, sinking heaviness of loss that can drive you into desperate longing for external gratification in such things as addiction, acquisition, and escape. But no amount of outward pleasure will ever satisfy an empty and unconnected soul.

⚛ You must open your heart to connect with your Divine legacy, the source of your receiving. After all, the joys of success, love, and real gratification can't flow freely *to* you if they can't pass *through* you. Once again, a shift of energy is required. Moving closer to the Divine necessitates retreating further from hate—whether it's dislike for yourself or anyone else.

An open connection requires you to consistently shift your intentions and make new choices each day. To open yourself up to God, let go of conflict, embrace peace, and always walk toward love.

The Divine Heart

The path to the Divine isn't a long road—just the distance from your head to your heart. Don't look upward to the sky, because your connection can't be found up there. Instead, meditate on your own heart center. Breathe slowly and deeply, and ask to feel the eternal light that already resides inside you. See it growing within and radiating outward, connecting you with all the other lights of Divine love. This is the nature of the vast soul of creation: We are all beams of that bright source, joined together in God's infinitely brilliant vibration.

In addition to daily meditation, another way to connect with this powerful presence is through sincere and heartfelt prayer. This has long been known to be a force of healing, protection, and inspiration, and it's also the conduit to the Divine. A prayer said with a genuine heart reaches the unknown recesses of the energetic world, often bringing results that nothing else could have created.

I keep a prayer list in the front of my journal, on which I place the names of people or situations that may need healing or resolution of some kind. Every day, I speak to God about those names; each morning and night, I spend some time sending loving intentions to all those situations. I focus on my own goals, but I also include more global issues, such as help for the homeless, healing for the sick, and peaceful resolution to hostilities. I also add an invocation for loving assistance to be sent to all those who have nobody to intercede for them.

Whatever you're praying for, your words and thoughts don't have to be formal or creative; they just need to be straight from the heart. Let yourself open the channels of communication when you want to release or need to heal; ask for what you want, and give thanks for what you get. Prayers of appreciation and thanksgiving are the whispers of love returned to the granter of all wonderful gifts. Express that gratitude in all that you do, and it will become a living invocation. When you see the Divine in every experience, you realize that your whole life can be a prayer.

There are many stories of athletes, inventors, financiers, rock stars, actors, and countless others who attribute their success to their relationship with God. Don't look at this merely as sappy sentimentality. The unlimited power of the Divine, the creative source and resonance of all the Universe, is your greatest supporter and the most loving, willing co-creator in your individual destiny. Open yourself to this connection, and you'll feel life-changing power in each and every breath. Great things can happen in your life, too—in fact, there's no greater achievement than a successful connection with God.

AFFIRMATIONS FOR LIVING IN DIVINE PRESENCE

- *I am blessed with the love of God. I am free.*

- *I release fear and self-loathing. I am safe and deserving, always living in Divine embrace.*

- *All joy, success, and peace of mind flow in Universal abundance to my life. Endless blessings come to me now.*

- *Every moment of Divine connection brings life-changing power to my life.*

- *I see the Divine in all people. Divine Consciousness connects us all.*

- *The love of God fills me up. My life is a meditation and a peaceful prayer. I embrace my own loving connection to my Source.*

- *I feel the power of prayer within my life. Through prayer and love, I connect with the immeasurable assistance of the Universe.*

⊕　⊕　⊕

PART VI

THE TWO OBSTACLES TO SUCCESS

Sometimes your pursuit of success seems to be met with one obstruction after another. Things just keep going wrong, your timing is off, the economy goes bad, or other things get in the way. You don't seem to make the right connections—or perhaps the people involved keep messing up.

These obstacles appear to be circumstantial. They seem to be outside of your influence and beyond your control, but don't believe it. You may think that they're merely coincidental, but they're really the energetic responses to your own personal resonance, and in this way, most of them originate with the self. In fact, the two greatest blocks you'll ever have to deal with are self-imposed. But this is good news, because you can change what you create!

Life is a process, a continuous stream of experiences—both good and bad. Energetically speaking, it's not so much what happens to you as how you respond to it that makes the difference. No matter what occurs or how long your success may take, you can choose to keep taking action, not only in the direction of your goals, but also in terms of your own consciousness and energy production. Whatever obstacle may arise, you need to remember that even a little shift in consciousness can create a significant—and even immediate—transformation in your life. Now and always, you have the power to make that change and see your goals blossom into beautiful reality.

✦ ✦ ✦

Chapter 26

ENGAGING IN LIMITING BELIEFS

The First Obstacle to Success

---

*"Believe that you will succeed. Believe it firmly
and you will then do what is necessary to bring success about."*

— Dale Carnegie

It's clear that your beliefs are the generator of both your energy and your destiny, so there's no greater factor determining your success. The two most damaging notions are conclusions of doubt and limitation. Just think about how the former affects your consciousness: Your brain can easily be convinced that what's merely perceived is actually real, so if you doubt that you can succeed, you'll create that in your conscious-ness—and then your consciousness will create it in your reality.

If you want the forces of the Universe to help you achieve what you desire, you must choose to live according to the Universal Laws. You could make all the plans and take all the action necessary, but if you have a failure mind-set, or even one of doubt, you simply won't be able to get the world to respond. If your energy is full of fear and limitation, you'll be fighting the flow, constantly struggling against the tide.

The real path to success comes from choosing strong, optimistic convictions. Everything about your consciousness creation is formulated in your beliefs. They're the source of your daily thoughts, which create your personal energy. Healthy cognitions create positive results; unhealthy ones create a damaging broadcast that invariably leads to unhappy outcomes.

⚖ The Laws of Magnetism and Manifestation are very clear: You absolutely will achieve what you believe—not what you want, desire, or hope for. There's no variation on this truth. Your beliefs are the fuel of the cosmic engine, your manifestation machine. If you embrace limiting assumptions, you'll project a consciousness of limitation and attract further restriction. But unlimited beliefs will produce boundless results and open your life to abundant receiving.

Blocking the Negative Pop-Ups

Think of your mind as a computer—when you type in a word or phrase and press the search button, you get a specific set of responses, and your mental processes work the same way. When you give your mind a certain word or image, it does a search for your most prevalent response. It's like a "favorites" setting or "bookmark."

For example, when you think of the word *job,* what's the first thing that comes to mind? What's the first feeling that it evokes? Next, think about the word *money.* When your mind searches for a response, what do you get? Many people have thoughts of lack and feelings of fear and discomfort. How about you? Now think of your goal. When you do a mental search, what do you find? Is it positive or negative? Does it bring feelings of excitement or worry and doubt? Finally, think of yourself, and note the results. If you receive any kind of negative response, you need to search again.

Your thoughts are like pop-up screens on the Internet. You could be going along, involved in a task, and suddenly have an unpleasant assumption appear. Sometimes it may be just a fleeting thought, but often the negativity is totally overpowering, filling the whole "screen" of your mind until it seems as if there's nothing you can do to escape it.

210

When that happens, you have no option but to shut everything down and reboot. You have to start all over with a new thought, and once you get one established, you have to be determined to block all the damaging pop-ups that may try to interfere. In fact, you can create your own positive defense. I've done it myself, and I've taught this process to clients who've used it in all sorts of situations.

POSITIVE POP-UP VISUALIZATION

Think of a positive image that's colorful, bright, and happy; it can be a picture of yourself looking wonderful, completing a goal, or engaged in a happy activity. Think of this cheerful image in vivid detail, and add a positive word or phrase to go along with it. Then, whenever you find yourself in a negative frame of mind, pop up that image.

Have it fill the entire screen of your mental vision so that you can't imagine anything else. Keep focusing on this picture until you notice that your unhappy feelings are changing. Breathe deeply and bring the scene even closer as you smile and relax; see every part of yourself in that reality. Hold on to this positive new image, repeating it as often as necessary until you start to notice your thoughts and feelings changing to a happier experience of yourself and your life.

This process will help you cement the new image, thought, and joyous sensations in your own consciousness—and in the Universal flow as well. It sends positive vibrations into the energetic realm, where matching energies will bring corresponding results. If you keep doing this every time you have a negative thought, it will only be a matter of time before a new dynamic energy becomes present in your life.

You can use this technique whenever you're engaged in a difficult situation or a doubtful or limiting belief. In fact, you absolutely have to! Your mentality creates your reality, so you need to choose a positive mind-set at every opportunity. Limiting ideas put walls around your resonance and block your success. Imagine what each thought of limitation sets in motion, since every one creates exactly the opposite of what you're striving for.

It's time to consciously reverse your old conclusions of doubt and limitation. No matter what you've believed in the past, you must rid yourself of these old, nagging thoughts now. You do have the power to let them go, and it's the only logical choice. Even if you feel compelled by habit or superstition, your negative beliefs will only churn out difficult results and get you absolutely nowhere.

Truth or Scare?

The following list represents some of the most common limiting beliefs regarding the issues of success, and these conclusions *don't* represent your truth. Such thoughts are not only energetically damaging, they're also harmonically destructive, throwing you out of balance with the Universal flow. To get back into harmony, you must believe something more honest and empowering. Stop deceiving yourself about your potential and start living in your power. Recognize the unlimited potential within yourself, your world, and all your personal pursuits.

Which of these beliefs do you find yourself engaging in the most? Identify the ones that you've had, and then write your new truths on index cards. Carry these with you and read them as often as possible. Add an optimistic image when you're reading—even if it's only you smiling and being happy. Visualize this picture, accompanied by your new belief, whenever you catch yourself engaging in a thought that you're trying to refute.

Limiting Belief: I'm not good enough (smart enough, attractive enough) to make it.

Personal Truth: I *am* good enough (smart enough, attractive enough) to succeed. I believe in myself and my ability to create a great future.

Limiting Belief: I need to be perfect. Everything I do has to be perfect. I have to be accepted by everyone.

Personal Truth: I accept myself. I can accept who I am and what I do without judgment.

Limiting Belief: How can I succeed? I've never really been successful before.

Personal Truth: I release the past and let it go. Today is a new day; this is a new thought. With every new moment I create a positive new energy.

Limiting Belief: I don't have enough money (education, luck) to succeed.

Personal Truth: I have all that I need to succeed. I have all the resources I need to create the great future that I want.

Limiting Belief: There aren't enough good jobs (women, men, opportunities) to go around.

Personal Truth: The Universe is abundant. There are plenty of wonderful jobs (women, men, opportunities) for everyone to have a successful and happy life. I am attracting those abundant opportunities now. There's always plenty for me to enjoy.

Limiting Belief: Things always turn out badly for me. If it weren't for bad luck, I'd have no luck at all.

Personal Truth: I choose to acknowledge all the good I have in my life. I am attracting more and more happy circumstances. I am truly lucky and blessed.

Limiting Belief: What I'm doing now isn't good enough. I have to do, make, be, and have more.

Personal Truth: What I am doing now is valuable and worthy, and so am I. I choose to see myself as successful right now. I see the value in everything I do, and I attract more to me.

Limiting Belief: I must constantly strive to be better. I can't accept myself just as I am.

Personal Truth: I am valuable just as I am. I don't have to do or be anything different. Every day, I choose to acknowledge my value more and more. I am learning to accept, believe in, and appreciate myself in every present moment.

Limiting Belief: I can't be happy until I succeed. I have to hurry to make this happen.

Personal Truth: I choose to feel good about myself and create happiness in my life right now. I know that a peaceful, happy attitude attracts greater success and joy to me, so I create that every day.

These are just some of the limiting beliefs that you may find yourself engaging in. Can you think of more? Jot them down in your journal and be sure to write the countering statements with them. Carry those positive thoughts with you and repeat them until they become your spontaneous reaction. This isn't just busywork; it's a crucial part of your positive energy production. The process of manifestation is so strongly linked to your thoughts and beliefs that you simply can't continue to engage in limitation without paying for it.

Blood Type: BE Positive

There are some people who actually define themselves through their limitations. Their negativity seems deep within their nature, in their very blood! They're so steeped in their own fears and anxieties that it never even occurs to them to respond in a positive way. Whether you engage in this type of chronic misery or only have the occasional fleeting doubt, you must use your power of choice to take a different energetic path.

Limited thinking is just another form of worry, and when you throw anxiety at a problem, the energy of that obstacle only increases. No amount of fretting, fear, or doubt will ever help create a solution; it just increases the difficulties you're already upset about. You must infuse your life with an affirmative way of looking at everything.

Changing your thoughts and beliefs may seem like a big task, but in the long run, it actually takes less effort to do so than to continue living under their negative influence. Do *not* look at this as impossible or even unrealistic. Limiting beliefs constrict your reality, and there's no getting past the energetic walls they set up around your pursuit of success.

※ It's your belief system that causes the most suffering in your life. It's not the dead-end jobs, the bad relationships, or even the lack of money—though these are the things you may want to blame. Instead, it's the hopelessness that comes from fear and judgment that makes you the most miserable. Don't stay stuck there any longer! When you finally make the decision to let go of despair, you can embrace the

truth of your unlimited potential. The joy and freedom that come from this will make worry a thing of
the past, empowering you more than you can ever
imagine.

I often relate an interesting story at my seminars that demonstrates
the power of belief. It's about a father who took his son to see the circus
back in the days before the arenas, when the show went from town to
town, taking the big tents with them. In one of these villages, a father
took his son to see how the workers set up the big top. They watched
as the elephants were put to work dragging the heavy canvases and lifting the huge center supports that were as large as telephone poles.

Naturally, the boy was amazed at the animals' incredible strength.
But later, when they went back to watch the circus, they saw that the
elephants were tied up. Each one had a rope around one ankle tied to
a wooden stake to the ground. When the boy saw this, he asked his
father why the beasts didn't just snap the rope or pull the stake out of
the ground. After all, earlier that day, they'd had the power to lift huge
poles and pull the heavy tents.

The father explained that when the elephants were babies, one
ankle was chained to a steel rod in the ground. Whenever they tried
to walk away, the shackles stopped them in their tracks, and they soon
learned that when they were tied down in this way, they couldn't leave.
This became their guiding knowledge and physical reality. Even after
they grew to a formidable size, they lived their entire lives based on
their baby-elephant feelings. Their existence was limited—not by their
truth, but by what they were taught.

What limiting thought is keeping you tied down? What personal
power are you dismissing just because you were taught at an early age
that it didn't exist? Whatever you've been told, you're more powerful
than you know. Best of all, you're unlimited in the ability to change
your thinking, and this gives you the ultimate strength: the power to
change your reality.

The Universe says "Yes!" to what you believe—whatever that may
be. Whether positive or negative, the conclusions you draw in your
mind invariably lead to the fate of your dreams and desires. Limiting
determinations restrict your outcomes, but when you choose to break

through your self-imposed chains and open yourself up to abundant belief, the Universe will say "Yes!" to the joyous fulfillment of your goals.

AFFIRMATIONS TO RELEASE LIMITING BELIEFS

- *I release all doubt. Whenever thoughts of limitation come to mind, I block them completely with a positive pop-up. I see my goal—close and complete!*

- *I release all worry and live in trust. I have all the power I need to make my dreams a reality.*

- *I believe in myself and my ability to create a happy and success-ful life.*

- *There is nothing that I can't conquer. I am unlimited in my power to change my thinking, energy, and reality.*

- *At every opportunity, I let go of negative thinking. I choose positive, trusting, and nurturing thoughts instead.*

- *The Universe says "Yes!" to what I hold true. I truly believe in my unlimited opportunities to succeed.*

⟡ ⟡ ⟡

Chapter 27

GIVING UP TOO SOON

The Second Obstacle to Success

"While one person hesitates because he feels inferior, the other is busy making mistakes and becoming superior."

— Henry C. Link

Many people never see success because they simply give up when the going gets tough. Real achievement takes time, energy, focus, and patience. Your willingness to persevere needs to be constant, because it may be the only thing that sees you through the tough times.

Modern Western culture has seen the rise of big wealth, and in some cases, fast money. It's a deceiving seduction that can lead you to grandiose expectations and unrealistic timelines. Although it may seem like a paradox to say, "Dream big, but be realistic," it's not. You should always have grand ambitions—and you should also be willing to invest the time, effort, and flexibility into making them come true. Be careful not to latch on to only one option or outcome, since this creates an urgency that sabotages the energy of your intention. You need to be persistent but relaxed, focused but flexible—both with your plans and with your goals.

I recently heard a good metaphor for this type of mind-set. Whenever a plane takes off, it has to declare a destination and file a flight plan, but sometimes things happen that may necessitate unexpected changes, such as bad weather or technical difficulties. The aircraft has to go around the storm or perhaps even land at an entirely different destination.

Your pursuit of success may take a similar turn. The destination is your goal, and the flight plan is your course of action. At any time, you may be compelled by circumstance, necessity, or inspiration to make some important alterations. Whether it's just a slight variation in your route or completely reconsidering your destination, you need to be willing to make the necessary changes.

In 1914, Bruce Ismay's goal was to have the fastest cruise liner across the Atlantic. There were warnings of icebergs, but no adjustments were made in the speed of the ship or its route. Far from reaching his goal, Ismay's brand-new, state-of-the-art ship, the *Titanic,* sank on its maiden voyage, bringing 1,500 passengers and crew members (and Ismay's business and reputation) down with it.

Don't sink your hopes and dreams in the icy waters of inflexibility and urgency. You may have to change direction—or even your destination—but if you're willing to reevaluate, reconsider, and adjust, you'll be able to see your destiny revealed. Stay open to the many options that the Universe has to offer, embrace them, and keep on going. Your determination will pay off!

Staying Power

There are countless cases of people who refused to give up in spite of difficulty and defeat. Here are just a few of them:

- After coming to Hollywood and playing bit parts, Clark Gable was told by a major movie producer that he would never have "leading-man" appeal. He went on to star in one of the most coveted lead roles in cinema history— Rhett Butler in *Gone with the Wind.*

- Nelson Mandela spent 27 years in prison. Upon his release, he rededicated himself to ending apartheid in South Africa. He received the Nobel Peace Prize and was elected state president in South Africa's first general election.

- Michael Jordan was cut from his high school basketball team.

- Stephen King struggled to make ends meet as his novels kept getting rejected. He worked in a laundry and eventually got a teaching job, but he got so disgusted with rejection that he threw an entire novel away. That book was *Carrie.* His wife saved it, and it became a movie and the first of many megasellers.

- The early works of Dr. Seuss were rejected by nearly two dozen publishers. After being accepted on the 24th try, his books sold millions and enriched the lives of children all over the world.

- Jerry Seinfeld was panned by the critics when he first started doing stand-up comedy, yet he went on to star in one of the most popular television comedies of all time.

- Guglielmo Marconi borrowed money from his family to develop wireless telegraphy. It was universally believed at the time that electromagnetic waves couldn't be sent past the horizon, so he was dismissed by the scientific community. It took more than six years, but he was the first to transmit transatlantic signals. He went on to win a Nobel Prize and become a worldwide household name.

- Conrad Hilton wanted to go into banking, but when his offer to buy a bank was rejected, he purchased a hotel instead. He slowly invested in several more, then lost all but one of them in the Depression. He was so deep in debt that his accountant pleaded with him to declare bankruptcy. He refused and went on to build a multimillion-dollar international chain of hotels carrying his name.

These are just a few of the countless stories of people who kept on going in the face of difficult—and sometimes seemingly unbeatable—odds. If you refuse to quit, your own story can join these; and your name can be added to the list of people such as George Washington, Charles Dickens, Albert Einstein, Florence Nightingale, Joseph Pulitzer, Abraham Lincoln, and Oprah Winfrey. These determined individuals refused to let adversity get them down.

The Bunny of Success

In recent years, an advertising campaign for a popular battery company showed a little pink toy bunny rolling through all sorts of challenging circumstances. Undaunted, the rabbit would spin on its heels and "keep going and going."

Your pursuit of success needs to be driven by the same kind of undaunted energy and intention. Where your dreams and desires are concerned, you need to be the bunny! To help you along the way, here are some strategies that can keep your intentions moving forward and your energy in excited action.

- **No matter what happens, never let self-doubt seep in.** There's no room for self-criticism or uncertainty in the intention to pursue success. Your consciousness and energy *must* resonate with confident determination—no matter how long it takes.

- **Always remember that your success doesn't depend on any one event.** Never make a single project or issue mean too much, because it creates desperate energy that pushes the desired outcome away. There are always alternative options, so pick one and keep going.

- **Don't be impatient.** Pace yourself and follow up on your plans while you enjoy the process—and your life. Your peaceful and persistent energy will do more to attract success than any individual goal.

- **Drop the conditional self-acceptance.** Stop comparing yourself to others, or being envious of them; those behaviors make you small and unattractive. When you live unconditionally, you attract in the same way.

- **Don't focus on what's going wrong; concentrate on what's going right and try to reproduce it.** When something doesn't work, let it go and renew your resolve to keep going.

- **Live in appreciation.** Notice, acknowledge, and celebrate what you have in your life. Dissatisfaction expands, so look around you and be satisfied.

- **Create a timeline, but don't set time limits.** If something takes a little longer, don't give up; just keep going.

- **Let go of regrets.** Wishful thinking about the past adds to resistance in the present. Stop brooding about old mistakes and look forward instead.

- **Get out of your comfort zone.** Take risks—do something new, different, and daring! Let go of your fears and take a chance.

- **Never define your setbacks as failures.** Failure has often been called just a high-priced education. When you learn what doesn't work, you can figure out what *does*—and move even closer to your dreams.

- **Be honest with yourself.** Be realistic about what you need to alter. Change can be safe and bring success, so always be flexible, open, and honest.

- **Keep your courage up.** Never see problems or setbacks as reasons to return to your old limiting beliefs. The Universe is abundant; face your future without fear.

- **Never lose your sense of deserving**. Whatever may happen, you still are worthy of having the best. Always acknowledge that, and be willing to do what it takes to make it happen.

- **Don't quit!** Keep persevering no matter what. Have faith, be open to wondrous opportunities, and look for a miracle. Better yet, *be* a miracle.

I had a gardener friend who grew a rare bamboo plant that took quite a long time to mature. The roots grew first, and then much, much later, the plant would come. She was diligent, though, watering the empty ground, weeding it, and even talking to it in order to nurture the plant that was on its way.

Her friends and family thought she was crazy because she did this for more than four years with no apparent results. They told her that she was taking care of empty ground, and they wondered why she couldn't see that the plant was obviously dead. But she kept going because she knew the special requirements of this species.

Finally, in the fifth year, the bamboo sprouted. In fact, it grew nearly 50 feet in the span of one year! All the time that she'd been cultivating it, that plant had been setting down roots strong enough to support its rapid growth.

Cultivating your success takes the same kind of diligence. *The work you're doing now is setting down roots equal to the size of your success.* So be patient, and keep going. If you create a sturdy foundation, your success will rise and be strong, abundant, and beautiful for all the world to see!

⊕

AFFIRMATIONS FOR UNTIRING PERSEVERANCE

- *No matter what it takes, I am willing to persevere.*

- *I am firm but flexible, determined and dedicated. I continue to act—no matter what.*

- *Any difficulty is just a new opportunity. I renew my determination and my focus at every turn.*

- *As I move toward my goal, I reevaluate and make the necessary adjustments. No matter what, I keep on going.*

- *I release impatience. I cultivate an attitude of success in everything I do. I trust and keep on going.*

◈ ◈ ◈

PART VII

THE ONE PATH TO SUCCESS

As you fall into a greater harmony with the Universal Laws of Attraction, you'll undoubtedly feel your energy shifting. You'll begin to notice your consciousness changing as well, and in time, the external variables of your life will follow suit. But the most important transformation will be the emotional quality of all that you experience, the pervasive joy that fills your life.

This process of flowing energies and attitudes creates a domino effect in terms of your manifestation. As you change your perception, you become happier, which shifts your personal energy; this will eventually alter what you attract into your life. In this way, the bottom line of continual and unlimited successful manifestation is the ongoing intention to create happiness in the here-and-now. So *be* the success you want to become; live with the joy you want to achieve. Don't wait a moment longer to embrace the attitude that your life is a blissful adventure—even now.

Chapter 28

LIVING WITH A JOYOUS, SUCCESSFUL CONSCIOUSNESS

The One Path to Success

"... exhilaration in life can be found only with an upward look.
This is an exciting world. ... Great moments wait around every corner."

— Richard M. DeVos

How has your day been? Were you as happy, peaceful, or joyous as you'd like to be? If not, what do you think it would take to make you feel that way? Take a minute to consider the answers to these questions right now, and write them in your journal. Be honest with yourself, because your success may hinge upon your answers.

Maybe you think that it would take having more money, more stuff, or perhaps a romantic relationship to make you happy; or maybe you believe that having a new job or a whole different career could bring you the joy and fulfillment that you seek. Be careful! These thoughts will only make you miserable in the present, sabotaging both your energy and your pure intention. The paradox is clear: Your conclusions about what you need in order to be content are actually destroying any possibility for real joy right now. Instead, you're creating an empty, aching consciousness of need that will prevent the very things you seek from coming to you.

- Don't confuse the acquisition of wealth and material goods with being happy. Energetically speaking, money doesn't bring you bliss. It's your happiness that brings you abundance! The delight that you already have in your life magnetizes those things that you think will bring more pleasure. This is actually good news, because with this attitude, you no longer have to wait to be happy. In fact, in order to create a truly successful consciousness, you can no longer delay the choice to enjoy your life.

But this can seem like hard work. Some people actually don't know how to be genuinely happy—they never saw it in their childhood or learned how to engage in it as adults. For these individuals, unhappiness becomes a way of life, and as strange as it may seem, the familiarity of that state creates its own kind of crazy comfort. This self-perpetuating misery may seem to be the path of least resistance, but it actually takes much more energy and effort to maintain a lifestyle of dissatisfaction than it does to learn how to become content.

The effort to create joy should never be attached to the achievement of your goals. Yet many people are so desperate for material things that they don't even expect or desire to be pleased until they're able to get just what they desire. This is a very childish and emotionally immature approach to life. It's the adult version of a kid saying, "I'm taking my ball and going home." If you don't get what you want, and you refuse to get into the game, you're isolating yourself from Universal flow and blocking the happiness that you'd be able to experience if you'd just let go and enjoy the moment.

This reminds me of an experience that I once had with my nephew when he was about three years old. I'd taken him to a restaurant, and while we were waiting for our food, he took out the action figures that he carried everywhere with him, just in case he wanted to play. Among them were some monsters and other gross-looking creatures, as well as about a dozen Power Rangers of various sizes and colors.

He began to set the Rangers up for their never-ending battle with evil, when his face suddenly got sad, and he frowned. He folded his arms in front of him and said, "I'm not playing." When I asked him why, he told me that he'd left his red Ranger at home. I pointed out that he had many other very strong and equally powerful combatants, but he still refused to play.

After a few minutes of silence, I said, "Okay, let's forget about that and play the happy game." To do this, we'd each take turns listing the things that we enjoyed. It always started out in a rather sane manner, as we'd list things such as snowball fights and hot-fudge sundaes. Eventually, however, we'd invariably break down into utter silliness as we listed things such as snot sandwiches and spider-gut soup.

My nephew loved to play the happy game, but this time he didn't budge. I tried to coax him into it by saying, "Come on, don't you want to play the happy game? We can get really gross. It'll make you happy!"

He just sat there and shook his head. Finally he said, "Without my red Ranger, I don't want to be happy!" He'd rather mourn the loss of something missing than enjoy what he had.

Surprisingly—and unfortunately—this response isn't limited to children. There are plenty of joyless adults who feel the same way. If they don't have exactly what they want, then they flat out refuse to be happy at all. Their grown-up versions go something like this: "If I don't have a husband, how can I enjoy my life?" or "If I don't get the money I want, I'll never be able to be happy."

Why is it so difficult to delight in our experiences? Why—in one of the richest cultures and most abundant periods in history—are so many people utterly miserable? The answer can be seen in two significant choices that we tend to make. The first is the decision to judge instead of value. This creates a sort of pleasure gap between our expectations of happiness and our actual experience of it.

Our second error is living in envy instead of appreciation. This can become a chronic, debilitating syndrom where our consciousness is focused on what other people have, causing our happiness to be eaten away by a gnawing resentment over what we lack.

⊕

The Pleasure Gap

People tend to look for fun in the extraordinary activities of their lives, often completely dismissing the potential for joy at any other time. This creates a greater and greater split between the quality of their daily routine and the experience of their more "special" times. Think of the consciousness that this produces concerning your day-to-day existence! If you only glamorize the unusual and dismiss the pleasures of the mundane, you can't help but experience a gaping emptiness for the majority of your lifetime.

The pleasure gap exists when you see relatively little value—and even less hope for joy—in the endless series of activities and tasks of life. With this attitude, you can only see living as a burden, a self-imposed negative definition that's guaranteed to make you unhappy, all the while projecting a miserable energy that will bring even more troubles to you.

You can find happiness when you choose to treasure *all* the experiences of your life. You can bring an attitude of playfulness—a fresh, lighthearted approach—to everything, including your everyday activities. This can't just be an occasional priority. It needs to be an overarching intention, one where you begin and end your waking hours in the energy of appreciation, no matter what that day entailed.

It's time to fill in the pleasure gap, bring delight to every moment of your life, and make all your experiences special. Always release the perception that life is a burden; it creates far too dark an energy for the Universe to have a positive response. Choose to look at your activities in an entirely different way, knowing that your path is filled with opportunities to experience peace, and always choose value—even today, even now.

There's an Eastern philosophy that says, "Chop wood, carry water." This simply means that all of life is a meditation, an opportunity to see peace and beauty in even the smallest details. This is the ultimate expression of the energy of appreciation, and it creates an easy, fluid consciousness that prioritizes present peace as the purest form of success. A poem called "Hyacinths," written in the Middle Ages, expresses this sentiment well:

If of thy mortal goods thou art bereft,
And from thy slender store
Two loaves alone to thee are left,
Sell one, and with the dole
Buy hyacinths to feed thy soul.

Hyacinths are my favorite flowers, and every year when I bring them into my house, they fill the place with the sweetest smell of spring. It's amazing how such a little thing can bring so much joy and gratitude! No matter what the season, you can always look around and ask, *What feeds my soul?* Think of the wonderful energy you'll create if you can experience all of your life with an attitude of peaceful appreciation. Your resonance of inner happiness will be downright irresistible!

The pleasure gap creates a huge polarity in how we experience life. It keeps us suspended in chronic all-or-nothing thinking, miserable in the belief that unless we're in a moment of rapture, we must be stuck in a meaningless void. We need to remember that no matter what's going on, the only time that joy can really happen is the present.

Bridging the pleasure gap doesn't mean the indulgence of physical desires in each moment; it's a deeper contentment, one that comes from a profound appreciation of the here-and-now. Real happiness is a choice—not something we simply fall into. In making the choice to be cheerful now, we create the energy that perpetuates that emotion always and everywhere.

In the London underground—the network of subways that move beneath the sprawling city—there's a sign that says "Mind the gap," warning people of the space between the platform and the train. It's time for you to mind the *pleasure* gap. Make sure that you're not missing real opportunities for peace merely due to your refusal to honor your life as being special every day. It's your choice: You don't have to wait; you can dare to be happy now.

The Salieri Syndrome

The movie *Amadeus* was a fictionalized version of the life of Wolfgang Amadeus Mozart. In addition to demonstrating Mozart's genius,

231

it relayed the story of a man named Salieri, a composer who was a contemporary of the title character. He was acclaimed at the Vienna court, but according to the movie, he felt very envious of Mozart's talent. In time, he became obsessed with this self-assigned competition, and it made him more and more miserable. He felt as if he couldn't compete with the beauty of the other man's compositions, and it ruined his ability to be happy.

Although historians disagree on the actual relationship between the two, this story is a great metaphor for the misery that a lot of people feel today—that is, the competitive attitude that engenders envy of those who have more. Rather than diminishing through the years, this emotion seems to be increasing and spreading to people of all ages and in all places. In fact, as more individuals become wealthy and their riches are displayed for all to see, it creates a *Why not me?* mentality. But wanting what others have eats away at your very soul. It translates into chronic, agitating dissatisfaction, a consciousness filter that can doom your intention for success.

Envy causes you to bitterly compare yourself to those who've achieved what you haven't. This self-condemning focus results in disappointment in the present and hopelessness about the future. It's the ultimate paradox that this obsessive concern with lack only increases it. The negative energy seeps into your consciousness, and can become a way of life, until all you can see is the emotional debris of constant dissatisfaction. Emotionally, energetically, and every which way, envy is an abyss of misery.

There's an old adage that says: "If you find yourself in a hole, stop digging." This is good advice when it comes to this wretched pit. If you already feel as though something's missing, this longing will only dig you deeper into that reality, but you can rise out of the hole by shifting your focus. After all, if that which you focus on expands, you certainly don't want to keep concentrating on what you lack and what others enjoy. Your obsessive focus on what they have actually creates the energy that sends more good things *their* way—not yours!

Instead, you can view others' lives and be happy for them. More important, you can look at what *you* possess and be pleased for yourself. You no longer have to hold on to the belief that you need more to be content. Instead, you can embrace the understanding that you'll get more as you welcome joy. It's your beliefs, not your material goods, that bring you pleasure.

If you're unhappy, it's not because you don't have the right job, car, or house; it's because you don't have the right attitude or belief. When you look around and feel blue, you don't need to change the circumstances of your life, just what you make those situations mean. You need to choose genuine appreciation for what you *do* have—right now.

This shift in energy is a critical step to creating a success consciousness. Stop being a prisoner of your own competitive moods; cease being a victim of longing and lack. You don't have to embrace the self-destructive premise that only certain objects can bring you joy. You have the power to end the envy and break free of the Salieri Syndrome; you have the option to enjoy the present and bridge the pleasure gap. It's time to let go of the desperate striving, the judgment, and endless competition, and to finally understand that your only point of potential happiness is in the present moment.

The Happiness Factor

Your consciousness is always in the process of creating! You need to direct its energy to the emotions and experiences you want, not the conditions you're trying to get away from. If you keep focusing on your problems, that's just what you'll attract—more problems. Instead, you must direct your attention to your solutions. Imagine the results, and visualize the positive outcomes, all while you're living with genuine happiness as your present point of view. This means that you have to get out of your own way and stop dismissing and denying the happiness you could already have. See the good things within and around you, and expect the Universe to send some more.

Success is a result of how you experience your process—not just in the pursuit of your dream, but in the routine procedures of your life. Behind every personal quest is the desire to find joy, but real achievement comes from doing that on a daily basis. *Happiness is the factor within the equation, not the product of it.* So, you absolutely must activate a joyous approach to your life if you want to create a dynamic success consciousness. This is so important that it must be the first thing you try to succeed at if you want to go any further.

A successful life has two requirements:

1. **You must be willing to let go of the things that are keeping your energy down and making you unhappy.** The two most important blocks that you have be willing to release are judgment and fear of the future. True happiness can't coexist with these kinds of thoughts and the emotions that they create. You must be relentless in your refusal to engage in these energies; so every time you catch yourself making a judgment, being self-critical, or envisioning a catastrophe, do an immediate intervention. Repeat: "Stop. Release. Breathe." Say this right out loud if you can, but at the very least, say it in your mind. Afterward, take a deep breath and let the thought go. Do this as often as necessary until your refusal to fear or judge becomes a spontaneous reaction for you.

2. **You must appreciate as much as you can about the present while continuing to work on your goals of the future.** This kind of gratitude comes from choosing to see the value of your entire life and your true self even now. You can keep moving toward your dreams, but you can't withhold your appreciation, waiting to bestow it upon some future event. It has to be given lavishly, genuinely, and unconditionally *right now.*

In *The Wizard of Oz,* Dorothy, the Scarecrow, the Cowardly Lion, and the Tin Man are desperately searching for the Emerald City. They're all looking for different things to make them happy, and they're told that the great and mighty Wizard who lives there can give them those things. When they arrive at their destination, they find that he's just an ordinary man hidden by smoke and mirrors and a frail little curtain.

In our search for success, we, too, are looking for the Emerald City. Like Dorothy and her three friends, we believe that the solutions we seek are in some far-off achievement, some distant, conditional goal. If we maintain those false assumptions, we'll set out on a journey where we'll be forced to face tornadoes of desperation, wicked witches of worry, and the flying monkeys of our own fears. We can still pursue that path, or we can choose to learn now what it took Dorothy a harrowing trip to find out: The solution is—and always has been—within ourselves. *Happiness is not a future event; it's a present choice. Success is not a specific outcome; it's a way of life.*

Having Fun in the Universal Playground

Something that really helps project the highest energy is having an attitude of playfulness when it comes to everything you do. This is a lighthearted and joyous intention, an approach that can bring a more high-spirited resonance to your life. Instead of looking at the day before you and seeing only endless drudgery, you can decide to have fun—and even play. Let go of your dread over doing the chores. What kind of energy does that perpetuate in your life? Instead of complaining about having to clean the house, acknowledge your appreciation for having a home!

> ⚛ Engage in your tasks with more creativity and enjoyment, and look for the beauty in your environment. Listen to inspiring or exciting music, buy yourself flowers, and dance and sing as you work. Remember that more than anything else, it's your daily energy that defines you—and determines your destiny.

If you can find absolutely no pleasure or value in the task that you're doing, bring joy to your mind by remembering something wonderful from your past or by reviewing your appreciation list. Recall a happy place, a fun time, or a special person, and bring renewed satisfaction into your life. Be more spontaneous and playful with your intentions. As you go through life, try to take things less seriously and less personally. Don't make everything be about you—especially the negative things.

Let go and live with joy. Have more fun in your life and you'll start to see a real difference in your attitude. The first time I tried to interject the energy of playfulness into my tasks, I was doing laundry. I'd always seen this as a real chore, so I wanted to change my energy around it.

Since nobody was home, I danced with the basket and started talking to my clothes, asking them if they had any ideas that could make this task more fun. I actually said this right out loud! Thankfully, they didn't answer, but this was kind of silly and fun, so I decided to continue. I proceeded to tell them that they were going to get a bath and feel so good after they were clean.

But then, when I was moving everything from the washer to the dryer, I realized that one of my favorite purple socks was missing. I held up the one I'd found and started interrogating it, asking, "What did you do to make your mate want to leave you? I saw you wrapped around that underwear!"

This made me laugh! I was actually doing the laundry and giggling. (Of course, I was also glad that my clients couldn't see me at that moment.) That experience not only changed that day for me, it also transformed my attitude about doing the laundry and so many other domestic chores. I realized that I could actually enjoy, instead of dread and despise, so many things that had seemed like meaningless busywork before. And while this may seem truly silly, it can completely alter your energy—so let yourself have some fun for a change!

THE QUANTUM TICKLE

Laughter is a monumentally attractive energetic vibration, and it should be practiced as often as possible. Studies show that this is one of the few activities that stimulate electrical impulses in all parts of the brain. In addition, it sharpens your thinking, enhances creativity, reduces stress, increases energy, and makes you more productive. Experiencing laughter on a regular basis increases serotonin levels and gives you a greater sense of well-being. It also sends positive energy out like a rocket!

So give yourself permission to let go and really whoop it up. Rediscover the child inside you. If it doesn't come naturally at first, trick yourself into being happy by faking a smile. Your brain doesn't know the difference. It will still produce endorphins, lifting your mood and changing your personal resonance. Most important, this will alter your perception—which shifts your consciousness creation. So let go of your old inhibitions and take the risk to have more fun. Laughter doesn't take a lot of effort, but it really pays off in creating a blissful consciousness and a happy, magnetic energy.

The admonition to cultivate light-heartedness right now isn't a cliché; it's energetic power. Living in joy raises your resonance and matches the very emotion you're trying to achieve through success. This entraining of emotional vibration is the most dynamic way to bring that achievement to you. The Universal Laws are clear: Your attitude about your life will shape it.

You have the choice to shape your destiny through pessimism or optimism, drudgery or enjoyment—and you make that decision many, many times each day. So set yourself to creating delight, and the Universe will respond with blissful returns. Always keep in mind that a truly vibrant consciousness of success is sparked by daily renewals of optimism, self-love, and joyous energy in the here-and-now.

Quantum Charisma

You are now—and will always be—in the process of consciousness creation. Construct a new, successful image of yourself. *Be* that picture—and believe it! Hold it close and clear, and revisit it every day. As it takes permanent shape in your consciousness, it will become your new reality. The journey to success is—more than anything else—an internal one. That's where your awareness resides and your energy originates; it all starts within.

When you think of people who have charisma, certain characteristics come to mind. They possess a joie de vivre, or joy for life, that infects everyone around them and everything they do. They have high energy, enthusiasm, and peaceful dignity that pervades their life. You, too, can create this kind of attitude now, completely changing the direction of your life. Your power of choice is your ultimate liberation—you can select joy, peace, and enthusiasm in every thought and perception. Since patterns of attraction always operate through the movement of energy, this is the highest vibration you can choose.

Your consciousness is your destiny order form in the Universal catalog, because it outlines just what you choose to prioritize the most.

Whether your focus is enduring lack or unlimited abundance, the Universe will surely fill your order, so never define yourself by the problem. Hold an unwavering focus on the solution. Remain single-minded in your determination to engage only in honoring and unconflicted thought, and your pure purpose will connect you with Divine intention and Universal flow.

Each and every change you make will alter your conscious direction, and even a little modification in consciousness can create a huge shift in your reality. The world is full of endless options, and the great field of all possibilities wants to send your dreams your way; stop resisting and open yourself to receiving. Your willing, self-loving intention is all that it takes to create an open, flowing channel to the source of all success.

When you align yourself with the Universal Laws, the sparks of success begin to fly. There's a current in the air that's quite literally electric. This is your quantum charisma—your relentlessly optimistic energy combined with a clear, conscious intention—and it's your most powerful force for successful manifestation. This pulsating power is with you at this moment, as is all the abundant potential that the infinite and unseen world has to offer. When you discover the bliss and beauty that is now and always within you, you'll have already achieved your *quantum success*—joyous appreciation for every moment of your life!

This present bliss is the beginning and the end of your success, and it's time for you to rise up to meet your greatest dreams fulfilled. Your destiny is already taking shape in the energetic realm. Witness the miraculous energy within and around you, and before too long a future full of miracles will unfold.

◈

AFFIRMATIONS FOR LIVING WITH A SUCCESS CONSCIOUSNESS

- *Every moment of my life is special. Joyous appreciation is my constant choice.*

- *Now and always, I am willing to change any negative, fearful, or limiting vibration. My present optimistic consciousness and my own happy energy are my greatest success.*

- *I see all that I do as an opportunity to succeed. Today I live with joy.*

- *I am happy, and I choose to bring an attitude of playfulness to my life. I smile, have more fun, and take more risks!*

- *I value myself and my life. I choose to affirm myself and see all the ways that I am successful now.*

⟐ ⟐ ⟐

AFTERWORD

The power of the Universe is your power. The light of the Universe is your light. The energy of all time and all space vibrates within your eternal consciousness, always engaging you in elegant acts of creation.

You're creating your future right now, diligently working at the destiny factory, churning out bits of energy, information, and expectation that will all be assembled into your own vehicle of future experience. It could be some cheap lemon that always needs to be repaired, or it could be a beautiful luxury sedan that runs like a top and gives you a joyous ride to magnificent destinations. It's totally up to you, because you're the one that builds it, assembles it, and drives it forward with every moment of your life.

For that reason, it's important to remember everything that we've discussed here. You live and move within the very real patterns of the energetic world, so don't dismiss it as too unrealistic. What's impractical is continuing along the same old lines if they haven't yet gotten you where you want to go!

Let yourself engage in this process for as long as it takes, and try to reread this book at different stages in your success pursuit. You'll find that different information resonates with you at each stage. Keep up with the journal exercises, and remind yourself of all the powers you have at your disposal. Three of them are absolute musts if you want to change the future you're creating now.

The Three Keys to Destiny Creation

All of the powers are vitally important in establishing a dynamic destiny, but there are three fundamental parts of your nature that should never be overlooked. In fact, they're so important that they

241

should be reexamined every day—even every hour or more! The following tips will help you use them to their fullest extent. As you go through your routines, always keep in mind these three central keys to destiny creation: consciousness, energy, and intention.

CONSCIOUSNESS

Your consciousness creates your reality, so you must be vigilant about only engaging in a positive awareness. The solution is developing a real knowledge of where your mental focus is all the time. When you concentrate on the value and joy in your life, those experiences will expand and keep on expanding to the degree that you continue to prioritize them. Remember these pointers to keep yourself on track:

- **Don't be a consciousness zombie.** Wake up to what you're thinking about and how that's going to impact your future. Only *you* can take control of what you're conscious of.

- **Keep reminding yourself of your consciousness options.** Never obsess about what's going wrong. Instead, shift your focus to what can go *right,* and lock on to that image only.

- **Always hold a positive perception of yourself in your mind and heart.** Whenever you get down on yourself, remember your new positive self-perception and loving definition of yourself.

- **Never be more conscious of what you lack than what you have.** Always make it a priority to acknowledge the good things that you are as well as what you have. In this way, you'll continue to manifest more abundance in your future.

- **Pop-up your options! Create exciting images of a happy and successful self and future.** Pop-up these image screens in your mind's eye several times a day. Make them bright, clear, and close; hold them in the center of your mind and breathe deeply as you experience their joy and excitement.

This will spark very real reactions in your neural pathways, neuropeptides, and conscious expectations.

- **Investigate your expectations.** Turn any pessimistic thought into an optimistic conclusion about future possibilities. Remember that the world is full of endless opportunities. Expect the best to come to you, and in time, it will!

ENERGY

You're always in the process of transmitting and receiving energy. Everything that happens to you is a return of what you broadcast at every moment. Even now, your thoughts, beliefs, and emotions are sending out very specific signals about who you are and what you're willing to accept in your life. If you want to attract successful situations and people who will help you create them, your resonance must vibrate with healthy beliefs, positive thoughts, and genuinely joyous emotions.

- **Always be aware that you're in the process of energy production.** Even if you're not conscious of it, you're still generating it. As often as possible, engage in the kind of thoughts and beliefs that generate positive and attractive vibrations.

- **Always choose to support, encourage, and believe in yourself.** The energy of confidence begins with self-honoring. Your choice to engage in thoughts or activities that are dishonoring to you invites the world to do the same. Success will never resonate with an attitude of self-doubt, so affirm your belief in yourself every single day.

- **Choose optimism!** There's absolutely no energetic value in a pessimistic outlook. No matter what's going on around you, you can look past the problems and open yourself up to receiving the solutions. Think about how well things could go, and then take action in that direction.

- **Find your real purpose.** Remember that part of your mission is to connect with your spirit, so let yourself learn more about who you are and why you're here. And once you've found out, honor that.

- **Stay present!** Energetically speaking, your power base is in the current moment. Remember that each new second offers a fresh opportunity to change your consciousness and energetic vibration. Even if you were filled with negativity just a minute ago, you can choose another vibration now. Forgive yourself, and let go of the past. Use the power of the present to manufacture a brilliantly beautiful future.

- **Live in love and deep appreciation.** These are the most attractive energies you can ever project. Send love to the people you're with and the projects you're involved in. Live with gratitude for all that you have and all that you are. Your intention to acknowledge and give thanks magnetizes even more to be grateful for.

INTENTION

Your intentions direct both your energy and consciousness, and as such, create the focus of your life goals. Real success is purely motivated, never driven by fear. When you pursue your goals in order to enhance a purposeful and joyous life, your intentions will direct the bountiful Universe to assist you in every way possible.

- **Never intend your goals to be the only source of your happiness, self-worth, or self-definition.** This is guaranteed to create urgency and desperation, highly toxic energies that will push your dreams away.

- **Consider your intentions seriously—whether they concern your professional pursuits or daily activities.** Give some thought to why you do things, and then ask yourself whether each intention is pure or fear based. If it's the latter, change either your action or your reason for doing it.

- **Make sure that you're not engaged in conflicting intentions.** If you want to succeed at something in particular, you need to be sure you really want it. Also, know that you deserve it, and believe it can be done. Don't cancel out your Universal order with contradicting doubts and beliefs.

- **Surrender any emotional attachment to your goals.** Let go of need, urgency, and desperation; be patient but persistent. Look for the satisfaction in the process, and you'll see real value in the end.

- **Live with conscious intention every day. Intend to live with joy!** Whether you're just doing some mundane task, or you're engaged in the pursuit of your dreams, do it with clear intention. Aim for value, peace, and loving appreciation.

- **Create a daily intention to connect with your loving source, the Universal Intelligence, the all-compassionate heart of God.** The more you make this living purpose an active part of your daily life, the more your energy will resonate in harmony with the abundant field of all possibilities.

Sharing Success

All three of these things—consciousness, energy, and intention—go into determining your own personal success, but never forget that your vibration also expands in the world to create the shared destiny of all humankind. The nonlocal nature of this influence means that you have power everywhere. In fact, your higher intentions have as great an impact on the success of our species as they do on your own life.

Every bit of energy that you project moves all of humanity in one direction or another—toward love and success or hate and destruction. Every thought of judgment or self-criticism accelerates the negative momentum in the world, while each caring focus accelerates the positive as well. Even just the intention to cease the struggle in your own mind works to end the conflict elsewhere in the world. This is the undeniable reality of the M-fields of shared consciousness: We're all constantly contributing to the consequences of our species, determining outcomes near and far. As each of us learns to vibrate on a more loving level, we'll not only unfold a brilliant destiny for ourselves, we'll also bring a higher, brighter vibration to the destiny of all humankind.

Good Vibrations

Remember to live an affirmative life. In all that you think and do, always consider your optimistic and nurturing options. Start with the statements at the end of each chapter, then add your own. Keep in mind that every present moment holds an energetic opportunity for you, so always choose an uplifting perception of yourself, your goals, and your world. Affirm your life every chance you get, and the Universe will respond in wonderful ways.

Don't dismiss this as some idealistic fantasy; it's a scientific reality that you really can't ignore. Your energy vibrates relentlessly through every single cell and experience. Your many options to resonate at a higher, brighter level never stop—not even for a moment. Right now, you can make a choice that has the power to change your life forever, so decide on an attitude filled with excitement, joy, and expectation. Rise above your old, unhealthy energy and resonate with a new belief in yourself and your unlimited world. Live with the image of your brilliant future floating all around you, and you'll find yourself immersed in that reality before too long. You design your destiny every moment of your life. Be the bliss you long for, and untold beauty and blessings will be yours!

✦ ✦ ✦

ACKNOWLEDGMENTS

I'd like to gratefully acknowledge and send my loving appreciation to the following:

- First, to the Divine Consciousness that lives in all things and loves in all ways.

- To my dear family: Sarah Marie Klingler; Benjamin Earl Taylor, Jr.; Vica Taylor; Jenyaa Taylor; Sheri Klingler; Devin Staurbringer; Yvonne and Earl Taylor; and Kevin and Kathryn Klingler.

- To the family of my heart: Barbara Van Rensselaer, Marilyn Verbus, Ed Conghanor, Julianne Stein, Melissa Matousek, and Tom and Ellie Cratsley.

- To my wonderful publishing family: Louise Hay, Reid Tracy, Jill Kramer, Shannon Littrell, Jessica Vermooten, Jacqui Clark, Richelle Zizian, Christy Salinas, Charles McStravick and *all* the lovely people at Hay House.

- To my office family: the ever-indispensable Noreen Paradise and the indomitable Rhonda Lamvermeyer, and to Karen Gray Price with great appreciation for the book.

- To my spirit family: Anna and Charles Salvaggio, Ron Klingler, Rudy Staurbringer, Flo Bolton, Flo Becker, Tony, Raphael, Jude, and the Holy Spirit of all life.

- Finally, to you the reader: Thank you for your light in the world. May God bring you happiness and abundant blessings always.

⊕   ⊕   ⊕

SUGGESTED READING

Ask and It Is Given, Esther and Jerry Hicks (The Teachings of Abraham). Carlsbad, California: Hay House, 2004.

Beyond the Quantum, Michael Talbot. New York, NY: Bantam, 1988.

The Biology of Transcendence, Joseph Chilton Pearce. Rochester, VT: Park Street Press, 2002.

Dancing Naked in the Mind Field, Kary Mullis. New York, NY: Pantheon Books 1998.

Elemental Mind, Nick Herbert. New York, NY: Penguin, 1993.

Energy Medicine, Donna Eden. New York, NY: Putnam, 1998.

The Holographic Universe, Michael Talbot. New York, NY: HarperCollins, 1991.

Intuition & Beyond, Sharon A. Klingler. London, England: Random House UK, 2002.

The Law of Higher Potential, Robert Collier. Tarrytown, NY: Book of Gold, 1947.

Molecules of Emotion, Candace B. Pert, Ph.D. New York, NY: Scribner, 1997.

The Power of Intention, Dr. Wayne W. Dyer. Carlsbad, California: Hay House, 2004.

Quantum Reality, Nick Herbert. New York, NY: Anchor, 1985.

The Quantum Self, Danah Zohar. New York, NY: Quill, 1990.

The Spiritual Universe, Fred Alan Wolf. Portsmouth, NH: Moment Point Press, 1999.

Taking the Quantum Leap, Fred Alan Wolf. New York, NY: Harper & Row, 1989.

✦ ✦ ✦

ABOUT THE AUTHOR

Sandra Anne Taylor has been a counselor in a private psychological practice for 25 years. She lectures throughout the world on the energetic laws of manifestation and the quantum mechanics of consciousness. She is cofounder of Starbringer Associates, a speaker and consultant agency that produces audio seminars for personal and business enhancement. The best-selling author of *Secrets of Attraction* and the nine-CD audio seminar *Act to Attract,* as well as several titles of guided visualization, Taylor is a motivating and inspiring speaker who appears throughout the United States, England, and Australia.

She lives in Ohio with her husband and her two children, who were adopted from Russia. She is cofounder of Forever Families Foundation, a nonprofit organization that assists families with the expenses and experience of adoption. Taylor actively advocates for foreign and domestic adoptions of older children, and she is the Ohio coordinator of Project Hope, a summer program that places orphans in prospective adoptive homes.

For more information—or to schedule a lecture, corporate seminar, or private consultation with Sandra, call: (440) 871-5448, or contact her at:

P.O. Box 362
Avon, Ohio 44011
www.sandrataylor.net
www.starbringerassociates.com

HAY HOUSE TITLES OF RELATED INTEREST